TALES OF WESTPAC

Memories of a carrier sailor of service
in the Western Pacific during
the Vietnam War

By

David K. Bowman, YN1, USNR (Ret.)

Vaga Books

Dedication

This book is dedicated to all my old shipmates from VF-194 and the USS ORISKANY (CVA-34).

Foreword

It should be noted in passing that, although the events and places in this book are real, all the names in the book proper have been fictionalized to protect the privacy of old shipmates.of old shipmates.

David K. Bowman

Table of Contents

David K. Bowman

Chapter 1

Alameda

The old C-118 transport plane, which had been in the air several hours after leaving NAS Miramar in San Diego, seemed to be flying lower than necessary that afternoon over San Francisco Bay. It was May 1969 and the personnel of VF-194 were being flown to NAS Alameda to board the USS ORISKANY for a cruise to Westpac—the Western Pacific. It was my first cruise, and what an adventure it proved to be.

For some ten minutes, give or take, I had been noticing our low altitude, but wondering only slightly. A few moments later, the co-pilot emerged from the cockpit of the aging craft, a stoic look on his face. His announcement made it clear that our low altitude was far from casual.

"We've had trouble with our landing gear," he announced, "and we nearly ditched a few minutes ago". Evidently they had vetoed it for some reason.

There was a moment of shocked silence, drowned out by the roar of the plane's engines. The co-pilot broke the silence to tell everyone that we were approaching the airstrip at Alameda and that they would attempt a landing. He cautioned that the landing gear might fail disastrously.

For the next several minutes, as the plane banked and dropped down for the landing, everyone on board sat silently, strapped into their seats, waiting.

Just then, the co-pilot returned from the cockpit.

"Alright everyone," he announced brusquely. "We're about to land."

Outside the windows, the airstrip rose towards the plane.

"Okay. Everyone lean forward and grab your ankles."

Most of us were young, inexperienced, scared. Everyone on the plane leaned forward and grabbed their ankles.

"We're about to touch down. Let's hope the landing gear holds. Everybody put your heads between your legs, lean forward--"

A lot of silent prayers were being hastily said.

"—and kiss your ass goodbye!" the co-pilot said, just as the plane touched down.

There was an outburst of nervous laughter that subsided into groans of irritation.

A moment later, before we had had enough time to become aware of anything else, the co-pilot announced that our starboard engine was on fire. Everybody out. We promptly complied, having had enough of that flight. Outside, a bus drove quickly up to collect us and take us to the pier.

The engine fire wasn't much to look at as we left.

Over near the pier, we disembarked from the bus, sea bagssea bags on our shoulders, and hiked the considerable distance to the USS ORISKANY. I've never figured out why they didn't give us a break and park closer. The government. Go and figure it.

The huge vessel loomed impressively along the pier, the Bay Bridge stretching towards San Francisco in the background. A gray behemoth, she was something like 900 feet long, her flight deck at least six floors from the water. Somewhere amidships, a large companionway arched from the hangar bay and across the water to the pier. We wearily made our way up the wooden gangway, each saluting the watch on the quarterdeck and requesting permission to come aboard. The Petty Officer of the Watch robotically granted permission and saluted each of us.

We had finally arrived on the ship that would be our home for the next six months. My own sea bagseabag must have weighed close to fifty pounds and I wasn't at all sad when I could leave it off in the berthing space. Amazingly, it would be thirty-four more years before I finally fell victim to a hernia.

Fortunately, although we were scheduled to pull out the next day, I had liberty that night. I remember I hopped a bus to San Francisco and visited the North Beach district. Back then, North Beach was one of the steamiest places on the West Coast, absolutely irresistible to a young sailor. The most lurid nightclubs were there, brightly lit, music blasting from their front doors, hawkers standing out front to pull in passersby from the sidewalk. Probably the most famous club on Broadway was Carol Doda's, with its huge neon sign of a dancing girl in front.

North Beach was definitely a sin-soaked, hard R--rated affair in those days. It has long since subsided into a somewhat seamy ghost of its former self.

I picked one of the most outrageous-looking clubs, I can't remember the name, and went in. Young, randy, bored, I wanted to check it out, because I knew it would be a while before I saw civilization again.

They made you buy two drinks as the cover charge, and then seated you. It was something else, like something out of a movie, with topless women in cages hanging from the ceiling or attached to the wall, dancing to loud music. I enjoyed it for a while, but it wasn't anywhere near as steamy as it was billed out front. After a while, I left and walked south on Broadway, until finally I began run out of business district, the buildings turning to apartments.

Crossing the street to start back, I found a memorable little bookstore. I've always been in love with books. It's long gone now—I couldn't find it on a visit to San Francisco a couple of years later.

This one was a doozey. It was your quintessential hippy store, but with a bit of a supernatural twist, with low candle light, flute music, and incense. I think the candles were black. An amazing place. They don't make them like that anymore. I shuffled around the store, peering at books, trying to read the titles in the flickering candlelight.

A short while later, I hadn't found a book that I liked and had had enough of the spooky ambience of the place. I walked back to the north to that little restaurant with sidewalk tables that they had used in *Bullitt* a few years earlier. Cute place. I can't remember much, but think that dinner was pretty good.

At the beginning of my second cruise, in 1970, I stuck closer to the ship, having a memorable visit to the large NAS Alameda Exchange and dinner at a nearby Italian restaurant. By then I had decided to take a portable eight track tape player rather than a record player. Our office was under the flight deck, right where the jets landed. Every time one landed, the whole damn compartment shook, which made the record player tone arm jump, scratching the record. That afternoon I got some smooth Henry Mancini tapes, most of which I still have, and which only get smoother with each passing year. That night, I remember that as I sat in the restaurant booth, I couldn't help but longingly think about my upcoming separation from active duty in October. Forty-one years later, I nostalgically look back at that night and wonder where those years went.

Next morning, the huge aircraft carrier cast off, steaming slowly and majestically to the north towards the open sea. Under the Bay Bridge, past Treasure Island and Alcatraz, the ORISKANY went, finally steaming under the Golden Gate Bridge. I went below to my workspace and by the time I stepped out onto a weather deck to have a look later that day, we were fully at sea, steaming west for all we were worth. Our next stop was the Hawaiian Islands.

Chapter 2

Pearl

I don't think I'll ever forget my first look at Pearl Harbor that misty morning when the USS ORISKANY turned slowly to the northeast past Ford Island. It was a still, warm morning in May 1969.

The huge ship slipped smoothly, steadily through the warm, clear water at less than 5 knots, the air heavy with the scent of hibiscus and fuel oil. Hundreds of sailors, one of them me, were "manning the rails" around the flight deck in their tropical whites. As we passed Ford Island, I looked down and marveled at what looked like large dark smudges on the airstrips and hangars, apparent signs of a recent attack.

"What the hell kind of housekeepers are they around here, anyway?" I thought to myself. "The Japanese attack was 28 years ago!" I would find out a short while later after I had gone on liberty that several weeks before our arrival, filming had completed on TORA! TORA! TORA!, a retelling of the 7 December 1941 attack on Pearl Harbor. Nuts.

The filmmakers were not only poor housekeepers, but during filming of the production, I heard, they were sloppy with their pyrotechnics, killing one or more naval personnel. More than passingly put off, the Navy Department had vowed they would provide no assistance with future productions. I couldn't blame them. It was bad enough to lose personnel somewhere in a rice paddy in Vietnam, but to have them blown up stateside in an incompetently staged movie explosion was comical.

Much later that day, I managed to get off the ship on liberty for my first exploration of Hawaii. The whole affair, in retrospect, was close to comical, too. Completely unfamiliar with local transport, and accustomed from my navy training to walking everywhere, I struck out on foot towards Honolulu. I should have checked a map first. It was something like seven miles from the naval station to downtown Honolulu.

Somewhere in my photo archives I have one or two photos taken near dark that day looking towards Honolulu at sunset. They don't' show that much, just the sunset reflecting off the bridge over the marina along the way. Shortly after I took those photos, I had my first taste of a Kona storm.

Kona storms are brief, drenching downpours that happen in Hawaii practically every day. Everybody there just takes them in their stride. Of course, they know what to do. A young sailor in tropical whites (short sleeve shirt, long trousers) out on a street at night is another matter.

Five minutes later, I was soaked to my underwear. I slogged a few more blocks and was in the downtown area of that many-storied port town, the home of the fictional sleuth Charlie Chan. Completely deserted and almost closed down for the night, it looked as though it hadn't changed since my Dad had been there in 1930. I almost expected to run into Charlie Chan.

The first place I would find that was open was the movie theater. I paid for my ticket and staggered wearily into the auditorium. However, my gratitude immediately changed to aggravation, as the building was crisply air-conditioned. Not a friendly environment if you're heavily rain-soaked.

I'll never know how I survived, but somehow I did. It helped a little that the main feature that night was "The Odd Couple." In the intervening years, I've become a great fan of that film. But it was a hell of an introduction to it.

After the film, I searched for a place to eat and found a dingy little café that looked as though it was old enough to have been visited by Amelia Earhart. After a desultory meal, I started out on the walk back to the ship. It was a long walk back, and I sank gratefully into my rack at the end of it.

The next day I had duty and the day after we were steaming for Westpac. That was my first taste of Honolulu. I remember that as the Duty Yeoman, I had to cut some orders for a shipmate whose marriage had gone sour and needed emergency leave. It happened sometimes, due to the separation of those cruises. Near the end of the cruise, on the way back across the Pacific, we made another stop at Honolulu for fuel and provisions for a quickie of an in-port period.

It wasn't until the spring of 1970, on the first visit of the second cruise, that I had a halfway decent experience in Hawaii. One of my brothers, who was stationed in Pearl Harbor aboard a guided missile frigate, had married a few months earlier. In February I had received a short letter inviting me to visit them the first chance I got.

The first chance arrived in May, when the O-Boat put into Pearl Harbor for provisions and fuel before leaving for

Vietnam. I arranged a three-day leave, which turned out to be, for the most part, paradise, Hawaiian-style.

My brother's new bride picked me up near the pier and we drove a couple of miles down Nimitz Highway to a quiet restaurant for breakfast. Following that, we had a beautiful drive across the southwest corner of the island to the little bungalow Taylor and his wife shared. It was located in an area usually reserved for locals on the west side of the island. Surrounded by lush tropical flowers on a narrow dusty road, the place wasn't more than three hundred feet from the beach.

My God it was a beautiful little place. I never saw a single bug while I was there.

We spent three wonderful days driving around the island in Taylor's convertible, enjoying the beaches, the food, Ala Moana Shopping Center. At night, we would end up back at the bungalow, telling stories, listening to records, eating fresh pine-apple, and drinking cold beer.

A shot taken of Waimea Falls during one of our outings in the late spring of 1970

I remember how on my last day there, we went swimming on the beach near the bungalow. It was near sunset when, amazingly, the temperature dropped just enough to actually raise the specter of hypothermia, probably somewhere in the upper sixties. In Hawaii. I couldn't believe it. We all scrambled for the shore, but the surf held a bracing grip on me and I wasn't sure for a moment if I would make it.

The last thing I felt as I made it out of the water was my U.S. Navy ring popping off my finger. I turned quickly and snatched at the receding water. Dammit. On a ruddy Oahu evening, I had lost the first of a number of Navy rings.

Looking back now, I wonder if losing that ring was an omen, as Taylor and his bride, Bonnie, divorced less than a year later. Bonnie checked out in a car crash in 1997. Taylor checked out by his own hand in 2009.

Those were the days, brighter, younger days. Life is such a rich tapestry of experience. But woven in among the joy and adventure is the pain and loss.

On the upside, in later years during my twenty-five year stint in the naval reserve, I had occasion to return to Hawaii many times. Oahu is still one of my all-time favorite places. It must be due to a combination of my experiences and memories there, the rich history of the place, the culture. Despite the commercial build-up and the Waikiki glitz, I am still very fond of the land of Kamehameha.

And there are also the facilities at Naval Station Pearl. In an effort to attract personnel away from housing off-base, the navy built a series of high rise barracks starting in the late 1970s or early 1980s. Each room has color TV and sleeps up to three. Just like uptown. Next door to Pearl is the Naval Submarine Base Pearl Harbor; they've got one of the best mess halls in the U.S. Navy, legendary. At breakfast they offer pancakes, waffles, omelets, all cooked to order, plus all the usual breakfast meats and fresh pineapple three times a day, seven days a week.

The officers on the other hand have a crumbling old building for a BOQ (Bachelor Officers Quarters) and only one dining facility, at Makalapa, across Nimitz Highway from Pearl, serving only two meals a day. Back in the 1980s during a training duty visit, one of the officers from my ACDUTRA (Active Duty for Training) group got ptomaine there. Poor slob, should've been enlisted.

On the first night of my first active duty for training (ACDUTRA) at Pearl in May 1976, after checking into the barracks, I went out looking for a place to eat. Sitting down on the bench at the bus stop, I discovered after a few moments of conversation that the man sitting next to me was a survivor of the 1941 attack. He was somewhere in his mid fifties, affable and matter of fact.

Before the bus showed up a few minutes later, he had related a hair-raising tale of that long ago Sunday morning at the Schofield Barracks. Lying in bed, he was suddenly awakened by the roar of approaching aircraft. Jumping out of his rack, he snatched for his trousers, hopped over to the door just in time see a line of bullets dancing on the ground in front of the building. He knew right then, he said, that this was not a drill.

Talk about synchronicity. How many times do you sit down on a bench outside the Pearl Harbor base and meet a survivor of the attack?

By 1969, the USS ARIZONA Memorial had been in place for ten years. Reached by a free launch from the old refueling pier on the east side of the harbor, it drew huge crowds. Ironically, I wouldn't see it up close until my first ACDUTRA to Hawaii in 1976. I can still remember staring pensively at the rusting, submerged hulk of the ARIZONA, and dropping a penny into the clear, warm, polluted water. The coin drifted languidly down to come to a gentle rest on the rusted metal.

By sometime in the 1970s or 80s, I think, a beautiful facility had been built across the quiet cove from the refueling pier. What a layout it was. At the entrance, to the right, leaning against a massive cream colored wall is one of the two-floor high anchors of the USS ARIZONA. It was awe-inspiring. The center boasted a gift shop, snack bar, museum and twin air-conditioned theaters. Visitors sat in one of the two lushly planted atriums to wait their turn to enter the theaters. Wired for stereo and fitted with semi-circular rows of comfortable seats, the theaters showed a short film on the 1941 attack, every fifteen minutes.

It's been many years since I first saw the film, but I can still clearly see it on the screen in my mind. First they would show footage from a camera skimming along the rail of the sunken ARIZONA. Voices would begin to intone from the right and left audio channels, in a near whisper, the names of those killed in the attack. Sudden cut to Japanese Zero planes circling Pearl Harbor, banking, bombs dropping and exploding. Cut back to the submerged wreck of the ARIZONA surrounded by aquamarine silence, voices whispering the names of the casualties. Quick cut back to massive explosions, huge plumes of black smoke, ships heeling over, Zero planes zooming overhead. Back again to the silent wreck of the ARIZONA, camera skimming along over one of the railings, fish darting by. Quick cut back to the ARIZONA exploding, dying, sinking. Then cut back to the underwater footage. Back and forth.

I don't think that you can see that film and still be the same again. The attack is particularly haunting to me. My mother used to tell me that when I was a baby, if a plane flew over the house, I would go into hysterics. Sometimes, I wonder if in another lifetime, I might have been there in Pearl on that Sunday morning, maybe on one of those exploding ships.

One time during my 1982 ACDUTRA in Pearl, I walked over to the new memorial center during my lunch hour. I went into the gift shop and almost immediately stumbled across a small pile of copies of "Baa Baa Black Sheep", by Colonel Greg "Pappy" Boyington. Casually opening one of them, I discovered that Pappy had signed it. A quick check showed that he had signed them all. As a seasoned book collector, I didn't need any further prompting, immediately purchasing a copy, which I still have to this day.

Semper Fi, my friend, wherever you are.

Chapter 3

Subic

My God it was hot, that first day in Subic Bay in June 1969. The word was that it was 113 degrees in the shade. I could believe it. The Mighty O, as it was fondly called, had steamed into the bay and anchored at the foot of the broad plateau that was the Cubi Point Naval Air Station.

The most frequent port of call for sailors in the Pacific, Subic Bay contained the largest complex of U.S. naval facilities in the hemisphere. Subic was also frequently the port that navy ships would make for if plans to visit other ports fell through. There was always Subic.

During this in-port period, the task was to take on provisions and prepare for a month of arduous duty on Yankee Station, our designated steaming area in the Gulf of Tonkin.

The Philippines was and is an incredible country of hardworking, friendly people who cheerfully confront grinding poverty on a day-to-day basis. Tagalog is the national language, but few people speak it, opting instead for Spanish, a leftover from Spanish colonialism, or their local dialects, which are innumerable. It was and probably still is a major frustration for the Philippine government that so few of its people speak Tagalog.

One of the first things that happened when the gangway was dropped into place on a navy ship in the Far East was that local vendors of books and other items were allowed to come aboard and set up shop briefly in the hangar bay. Among the vendors who came aboard were locals who picked up laundry for those wanting a break from the punishing apathy of the ship's laundry. A favorite service they offered was the embroidering of a sailor's name on desired garments—front of the chambray shirt, rear of the dungaree pants, work jacket, so forth.

When we came into port, it was always welcome to be able to pick up a couple of books and send out half a dozen pairs of work shirts and pants so that you would look sharp for the next couple of weeks. I still have a few paperbound Charlie Brown books for keepsakes that I bought back then on the hangar bay during Westpac cruises.

Standing in the hangar bay that first day in the Philippines, I looked across at the pier, at the people, the equipment, and the vehicles, at the Filipino taxis waiting for the flood of business they would get when liberty was called. I was fortunate to be in the liberty section, and could hardly wait.

During the steam from Honolulu to Subic, I had acquired what seemed to me to be the worst case of heat rash on the ship, and possibly the whole Seventh Fleet.. What had brought this about was that there were no air-conditioned spaces aboard the ORISKANY for enlisted men, outside of spaces with technical equipment, which had to be air-conditioned. Air conditioning was almost completely reserved for the officers. We slept, ate and worked in unremittingly hot spaces. Only the weather decks or our occasional duty in ready rooms offered a respite from the brutal heat.

I had been urged by the corpsmen in the sick bay to get some sun once we had gotten into port, that that would help clear up my heat rash. Given my inexperience with the tropical sun, that turned out to be disastrous advice.

A while later, liberty was called and we all filed past the petty officer on watch on the quarterdeck, saluted and requested permission to go ashore. Coming down the after brow, I was hit by a wall of moist heat, the smell of fuel oil.

Flagging down a Filipino taxi, I fell into its air-conditioned refuge and heaved a huge sigh of relief. God it was hot. I went straight to the base pool to cool off. Once there, I splashed and paddled, lay out on the side of the pool for a while. But after about 45 minutes, I began to feel ill. I staggered into the locker room, had a shower, dressed, and finally left for the base theater. I still wasn't sure what was happening.

After about 20 minutes in the cool darkness of the theater, I was still feeling badly and couldn't take it any longer. Marching into the restroom and staring into the mirror, I couldn't believe what I saw. Jesus. I looked like the *Plat Du Jour* in a seafood restaurant. I was beyond well-done. Not long afterward, I hopped another cab, returned to the ship and made it to sick bay. Unimpressed, they handed me two aspirins and a bottle of Calamine lotion. In those days, they could discipline you for getting sunburn. I barely made it down to my rack and collapsed.

Two of my shipmates in the squadron office, Harry and Jeff, (not their real names) had even worse luck the following year during my second cruise. Harry and Jeff were very much like Hawkeye and BJ from the old MASH TV series, and were noted for their zany antics.

There was an island in Subic Bay the navy called Dungaree Island where sailors could literally go on liberty in dungarees. The island boasted all sorts of recreational facilities, including an enlisted men's club.

One fine day, during an in-port period, Harry and Jeff went on liberty to Dungaree Island. They drank liberally in the club, got reasonably soused, and then found themselves a place on the beach to fall asleep. Unfortunately it was a bright, hot, afternoon, and the tropical sun was merciless.

When I saw them the next morning, they were a sight. They had slept for hours in the sun, with their pants rolled up, their arms exposed in short-sleeved shirts, and their Dixie cup hats jammed down on their heads.

That morning they reminded me a little of a pair of hung over baboons, their faces red from the brow down. Their forearms and lower legs were also badly sunburned, and every movement was agony. Poor guys. I felt sorry for them. They were good lads and quite fine as long as they didn't imbibe. I occasionally still think of them.

Speaking of lost nights, almost every sailor has his share of them. This is particularly true of Westpac sailors. After a month at sea, the majority of them make a beeline for the various clubs and dining facilities on base and off. In the Philippines, they were sure to venture, sooner or later, to the nearby town of Olongapo for diversion.

Olongapo's streets were crowded with countless bars and clubs that catered to U.S. military personnel. The clubs were staffed by local Filipino b-girls, who, with the chill air-conditioning, loud music, and beer so cold you couldn't taste it, provided an irresistible attraction for sea-weary sailors. Myself included.

I can still clearly remember those lost nights in dark, air-conditioned clubs, and the Filipinas on my lap, sometimes guiltily wondering what eventually happened to them, because I was able to go home after my active duty. They stayed behind to struggle for a living in their corrupt, poverty-stricken country.

I can remember that on what I think was my first visit to Olongapo, I encountered a vendor who sold monkey meat on sticks. Nearby tottered an apparently drunk Filipino, carrying a stick of monkey meat. Suddenly he lost his balance and fell over, staring up beseechingly at me in the ruddy glow of a nearby light. I looked down helplessly at him and walked on. Nearly forty years later, I still remember that surrealistic scene and wonder what happened to him, wonder whether there was something I could have done.

Below is a view of one of the sweetest sights in the world to a sailor at the end of a long day ashore:

The after brow, or gangwaygang way.

Another thing that sailors occasionally encounter wherever they go is local folklore. Subic is steeped in its own unforgettable brand. I encountered one memorable example late one hot, quiet afternoon, in of all places the Cubi Point Acey-Ducey Club (for First and Second Class Petty Officers). There were two fellow squadron members with me at the table, and somehow, the subject of local folklore came up.

One of my friends related a story told to him by a Filipino cab driver about a nurse in the nearby naval hospital. It was in the early 1940s, just after the Japanese invasion of the Philippines. The nurse had recently had a baby, over which she doted. Soon after the invasion, the Japanese separated the nurse from her baby and she became inconsolable.

It's been many years now since I heard the story, but as I recall, the fate of the nurse was not clear, nor that of her baby. However, from time to time, her ghost is seen on the hillside below the hospital, still searching for her baby.

On a number of occasions, I traveled up and down that hill in cabs during visits to the base. The road up the hill was narrow and winding, with deep jungle crouching on either side. At a couple of places, a street lamp broke the darkness, casting a pale, unreassuring light over the silent jungle. Drivers never paused for a moment on that road.

Subic Bay was the scene of a brief vignette I have never forgotten. It involved a good fellow, a third class I think, who had the misfortune to be named Larry and have a polish last name. He had been dubbed in good fun, for better or worse, Lawrence of Poland, after the Peter O'Toole film, which was popular then.

We had been called to muster on the hangar bay a day or two after our arrival in Subic somewhere in the middle of the '69 cruise. The commanding officer stepped up in front of everyone to make a brief speech, about flight line safety.

"Yesterday, we almost lost Lawrence of Poland," he began with a soft smile. There was brief chuckling, then he went serious. "We've got to pay attention and be safe out there", he went on, describing how Larry had been standing in front of one of the F8J's on the airstrip at Cubi. The engine on the jet fighter was going full tilt at the time. Ill-advisedly Larry turned his back on the jet and soon found himself walking backwards towards the intake.

Before he knew what was going on, the hapless plane captain's safety helmet was suctioned off his head and blew loudly threw the engine. Fortunately, before Larry could follow his helmet through the engine, the very alert pilot shut down the craft.

The navy's concerns here are twofold: They not only do not want to have people injured, but it definitely spoils their day when foreign material is blown through a jet engine. They call it FOD. Foreign Object Damage.

A big deal is made of policing the area where jets are parked, the flight line, for the smallest piece of material. I learned immediately on the first cruise that something as small as a cigarette paper can royally screw up a jet engine. When that happens, they have to pull the engine and leave it off at a shop in Subic the next time they're in port for a huge overhaul, costing thousands of dollars.

"We've got to be more careful," the CO summed up. "We can't afford for anybody to get hurt." He made a few more remarks, and then we were dismissed.

As it was about lunch time, I went below two decks to the mess deck. A short distance from the double ladder leading down to the messing area, who should appear from a hatch on my left but Larry, carrying what looked like a hundred pound bag of potatoes. I say hi to him and walked on. They'd evidently given him a little KP for a change of scenery. He was back on the flight line eventually. The navy was always good about second chances. That's one of the things about them that I always liked.

Another time at Subic, somewhere during the summer of 1970, a flap happened that was memorable and illustrative of how mistakes can happen.

On quiet evening when I had the duty, the "General Quarters" alarm sounded. When you're underway you go to "battle stations". This time, the entire duty section, hundreds of people, were ordered to shore immediately. There was a fire spotted atop the nearby plateau of Cubi Point Naval Air Station.

Hundreds of men clattered through the ship, across the hangar bay and down the after brow. By the time we had reached the pier, many of us were puffing. Unhesitatingly, we made for the steep embankment that sloped up to the airstrip. By this time, overweight chiefs and firsts were really out of breath, fighting to get to the top.

As the first people made it to the top of the slope, here arose a chorus of angry shouts and grumbling that only got louder for a few more moments. The "fire" turned out to be the fuselage of an old plane propped up on a wooden stand in a controlled burn. Firefighting school. Sonofabitch. There were some very upset chiefs that night. But what are you going to do? The hillside was steep and the lookout on the bridge just couldn't see everything. Just the ruddy glow of the controlled burn.

Well, at least we should have gotten some physical fitness points for that one.

Chapter 4

The Land of the Iron Butterfly

I had a couple of memorable of excursions into the land of the Iron Butterfly, as Madame Marcos, wife of President Marcos, was called in those days.

During the summer of 1969, the chief in my office very graciously invited me with him on a short leave to visit Angeles City, his hometown, up north toward the center of the island, not far from Clark Air Force Base. Loving travel and being anxious to learn more about the Philippines, I readily accepted. A short time later, in July, we docked in Subic and the chief and I took off.

The mode of transit was typical for the Philippines and the World in general—a rundown bus filled with not only people but chickens and goats and anything else that they thought they needed to bring on the trip. Sanitation was, of course, preposterous. We set off on a bright and sunny morning, rumbling our way through jungles and farmland, up hill and down. all too frequently passing the quintessential wooden house raised off the ground on ten foot poles. The poles were probably to help escape flooding and insects that must have been *de rigueur* in that part of the world. One feature of the Philippine hills I have forgotten was their rounded tops. I remember clearly at sunset the first day of the trip reaching the top of a hill and seeing the rounded hilltops stretching into the distance.

Finally, the next day, we reached Angeles City and were met by the chief's family. They had two houses side by side, one of the traditional Filipino design with no electricity or plumbing and the other one up to western standards, where they billeted me. In the kitchen was a glass-fronted cabinet in one corner, filled with goods from the U.S., including a six pack of Coca Cola, none of which were ever touched. I'm sure they were there to show that the household was up to western standards.

My stay there was short but memorable. The first night there they took me to a Filipino night club that featured excellent music and racy entertainment. Eventually, I was returned to my quarters, where I turned in on a comfortable bed covered with insect netting and for good reason. My night's sleep started out warily when I heard something immense buzzing not far from me for some long moments. I was appalled, as it sounded like a small buzz saw. And, indeed, the next morning I discovered that I wasn't too far off the mark: On the bed next to mine was a three inch long fly. My God, it stills makes me shudder to think of it today.

Later that morning, my friends took me out to see the shops, stopping at a tailor, who measured me, and by that afternoon he had created a pale yellow jack-shirt for me that fit perfectly. I wore it on the trip back to the ship the next day and have it to this day.

Some images taken during the trip, mostly in Angeles City.

Later that same day, we were briefly out at Clark Air Force Base. I think I sat in the car while someone took care of an errand. We may also have visited the Base Exchange, although it's hard to remember after nearly 43 years. It was an innocuous enough visit, but enough so I remembered the base, and was properly awestruck when I hear the news years later on June 15, 1991 that Mount Pinatubo had erupted disastrously. It was a bit surprising to learn that the U.S. Government had opted to abandon the base in the face of the cleanup costs. I wonder if the place is still one huge ash pile, for, if the cleanup costs were daunting to the U.S., they must have been outright overwhelming to the Filipinos.

The next year, 1970, in the summer, when we docked in Subic Bay, the ship's chaplain offered another of those wonderful and impossibly affordable tours, this time to Manila. It consisted of a bus ride to manila and one or two days at a very nice hotel, which turned out to be stated along Manila Bay. Romantic, you say, until I have to mention the aroma of sewage wafting in on the evening air.

Oddly, when I looked out of my window, I could see Filipino children playing in the surf.

I remember that the first evening there, we were taken to a very elegant restaurant. Outside were a group of Filipino children playing on the sidewalk. My appetite was not stimulated much, however, by the huge bug there were cheerfully playing with. I did my best to forget quickly as I entered the restaurant, which had multiple levels and a large fireplace in a wall of grey stones.

The next day, was as good as it gets. I had a Filipina as a guide and we spent the day exploring Manila. Among other places, we visited the Presidential Palace, which was resplendent in the trappings of the Marcos wealth: elegant furniture, beautiful paintings, sumptuous wall hangings, carpets. To this day I'm mildly surprised that they had the place open for tourists. Perhaps the ability of everyone to see the opulence in which their president and his wife were living helped to foment the later revolution in 1986 that ousted Marcos.

There was also the new Manila Cultural Center, built my Madame Marcos at a cost of about $4 million pesos. Back then that would have been one million US dollars. In any event, its construction caused some consternation and brought some criticism, as the city seemed to have a much greater need for sewers, electricity and other infrastructure. To bring it into perspective, even in 1970, when one went two blocks .back from the graceful row of hotels along the bay, one encountered complete slums. Manila was, in fact, a huge slum, candy coated with rows of beautiful hotels and occasional broad parks.

One such park was Jose Rizal Park, large and graceful, with a scenic fountain in the middle.

What follows are images of Rizal Park and the Cultural Center.

Jose Rizal Park

Philippine Cultural Center

Dr. Rizal was and is the national hero of the Philippines, as the result of the remarkable courage he showed during an attempt at revolution by the Filipinos in 1895. He was kept prisoner in Fort Santiago by the Spanish for a long time and then later shot in 1896. It was one of the stupidest things that the Spanish ever did, although not by much, if you look at the history of Spanish colonization in Mexico, Central and South America in the 1500s. Coincidentally, on the city tour that I took, I visited the fort, which is still more or less intact and quite colorful. Part of the tour included going up a flight of stairs to a small, dingy room where Rizal had been imprisoned until his execution. Amazing place. It was a moving experience.

Fort Santiago

Before we were done, we had even stopped at the Chinese Cemetery at the edge of town, noted for its opulent memorials and crypts.

It was with some melancholy that I bid farewell to Manila the next day.

Chapter 5

Tonkin Gulf Yacht Club

We called ourselves the Tonkin Gulf Yacht Club. I used to have a nice blue working jacket with a large circular patch on its back emblazoned with that motto. On the front, on the left breast, I had had my name embroidered by a Filipino laundry. On the right breast was a circular squadron patch, bearing the unit's trademark lightning bolt. Shortly before I was helo-lifted from the ship to DaNang in September 1970, some sonofabitch stole it from my duty station in the VF-194 ready room. I've tried my best to forgive and forget, but somehow it still occasionally rankles.

The main cruising area of the Tonkin Gulf Yacht Club was a large area to the east of Vietnam, where carriers steamed in a huge circles, launching their various aircraft on missions. Yankee Station. But what those missions were was a mystery to all but those with a "need to know".

The ready room, just down the passageway about twenty feet from the squadron office, was the nerve center of the unit. It was were all officers went for briefings prior to launching on missions. And carrier duty is the most dangerous there is navy for pilots. Like landing on a postage stamp. I once saw an example of the danger involved. One day I went into the ready room to do something and noticed one of the officers, a lieutenant, had a large dark bruised area on his face. He looked like he had been hit in the face with a monkey wrench. When I got back to the office, I asked a shipmate what had happened to the Lieutenant, whose name doesn't need to be mentioned. I promptly found out. When the lieutenant took off on a mission, he loosened his harness. Returning to the ship later that day, he forgot to re-tighten his harness before his arrested landing on the ship. When his plane stopped aboard the ship at 250 knots, his face didn't. Right into the control panel. Ouch. That's gotta hurt.

We were frequently in the hostile fire zone and close to the action. I can remember being above decks on a number of evenings and being able to see the flash of ordnance a mile or so away, onshore. It was fortunate that it never occurred to the enemy to attack us. But then, attacking an aircraft carrier is a lot like attacking a hornet's nest, and you've got to be able to deal with the hornets.

The closest we ever came to seeing any opposition in the air was very infrequent flyovers of Russian aircraft, about once a cruise. "Red Bear Flyovers" they were called. We were always ordered to stow away all cameras. I was never quite sure why. They were far too high and I was never interested in photographing them.

The first day or two out of port was always cathartic. It was a relief, at least for me, to be out on the quiet sea with its balmy breezes, after a week of bright lights, loud bands, partying. But after a couple of weeks everything settled into a dull tedium. The fresh food would all be gone and we would live off of powdered everything and coffee that tasted as though it had been pumped from the bilges.

Jesus, what coffee.

But I actually became inured to it after a while. And the pudding they served to us earned a special nickname from me: "wall paper paste". My God, what a concoction. But they tried, they did their best. It was just that technology wasn't what it is today, and they just didn't have some of the great shelf-stable foods they have now.

A major source of recreation when off duty was for personnel to go up the 02 or 03 level on the superstructure and watch flight operations. Over a period of two cruises to Asia, I saw a lot of operations, both by day and by night. It was always impressive to watch those great metal birds going through their paces.

An F-8J Crusader jet is an awesome machine to be around when its engine is running. Since military jet engines are not muffled, it's like the thunder of Almighty God. Mufflers reduce available power, and power is the name of the game. It's particularly loud just before takeoff on a steam-operated catapult, when a jet has its engine turned up to full power, standard procedure to insure a safe takeoff.

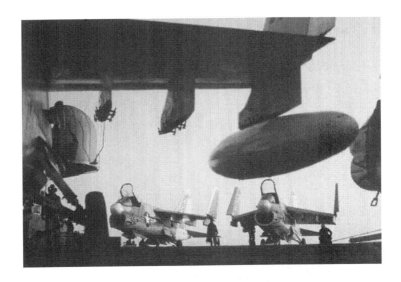

Stand down

Bolter!
(A bolter is when the landing is deemed to be unsafe
and is cancelled. The pilot then makes another approach.)

Recovery!

One of our (VF-194) F8J Crusaders launches

One of VF-194's jets readying for launch

A landing by an A-7

The one prop plane on board the Big O, our beloved COD, or Carrier Onboard Delivery, which was used to fly mail and personnel aboard.

I can't tell from this one whether they were picking up FOD or playing craps!

Players from a USO show held in the aircraft elevator

An A7 comes in for a landing.

Even with the hearing protection they made you wear, it was still hard on the hearing. I used to worry how the plane captains on the flight deck managed to avoid going deaf.

They probably didn't, and to this day, I have a hearing deficit as a result of being around jets.

So you stand on a steel balcony watching either forward towards the launching jets, or back aft towards the ones that land. Night takeoffs are especially spectacular, as all you can see is the glowing red orb of the afterburner, soaring into the night sky amid a deafening roar.

Day operations are even better, as you can see more. The most spectacular photo I got during my two cruises was one of a jet boltering past the superstructure.

Boltering refers to aborting the landing and continuing forward, back into the sky. Landings aboard carriers are accomplished by huge hooks on the tails of the aircraft, which catch on big cables stretched tautly across the flight deck. The Landing Signal Officer keeps a sharp eye on all approaching landings and is not bashful about aborting one. Amen to that. A mistake in an arrested landing can cost lives, cause injuries, wreck equipment, and, in general, raise holy hell. The navy always tries to play it safe.

I remember that we once had a net landing. A net landing is where the pilot can't get his landing gear to deploy, so a net is stretched across the flight deck. The jet comes in, then the pilot cuts the power and does the best he can to slide into the net and stop. I couldn't get away from my duty station that day to see it, but fortunately no one was hurt and the damage was minimal.

The most legendary and horrible type of accident is a ramp strike. It's just like it sounds. An approaching jet comes in too low and strikes the jutting edge of the flight deck, or ramp, as it's called. Thank God they don't happen often, as they usually cause injuries, death, and damage. We never had one during my two cruises.

We did have a few small losses. I know this because there was something about my face that the squadron's Leading Chief didn't like. He was a good fellow, a bit stoic, though. Whenever you encountered him and asked him how he was doing, he would reply noncommittally, "About average."

I was assigned to every memorial ceremony they held during those two cruises.

The most elaborate ceremony was for a pilot from one of the other jet squadrons. During a mission one day, he became so distracted, or possibly so clinically detached, that he forgot to pull up at the end of a pass of some sort. He flew right into the ground.

The ceremony was held on a beautiful clear day. As usual, the marine color guard was there. That seemed to be one of their main jobs on the ship. Also, all of our task force, something like five ships, steamed impressively abreast, at something like 20 knots, flags flapping in the sea breeze, and hundreds of sailors manning the rails on all their decks.

For a quite a while, the vessels steamed along side by side in relative silence. I was in a large group of perhaps 300 sailors and officers standing at endless attention in increasing discomfort. The only sound, when nothing else was happening, was the distant whine of the ship's engines and ventilation systems.

This ceremony was far more elaborate in that personnel from the ship's photo lab circulated around, taking not only still photos, but also movies. On a table near the color guard, there was an audio tape deck, recording everything that occurred, the chaplain's speech, the prayer, the thundering three round rifle salute.

Finally, at the end of the ceremony the flag was lowered, folded and placed in a special glass-fronted case. The photos, movies, tape recording and folded flag would be transmitted to the deceased officer's family. A class act.

Another ceremony was precipitated by the loss of a young sailor. I can still remember that call to general quarters that night long ago. General quarters was and is called not only in battle situations, but in most significant emergency situations. I clattered out of my rack, pulled on some pants and boots and dashed down the passageway to my general quarters station, the squadron office.

Over the 1MC (loudspeaker), a "man overboard" alert was passed. The Leading Chief took a head count in the office and we all remained there while head counts were taken all over the ship, 4500 of them.

A week or so before, a nineteen-year-old seaman apprentice had gone missing. The captain was inclined in such situations to come on over the 1MC to talk about it. It was actually a bit comical. The kid had been missing for half a day or so. I remember the captain saying, "Come on, son. Come out from where you're hiding and we'll talk about it. We won't hurt you. We've got helicopters circling the ship looking for you." And they did, so help me. "We're searching the ship for you." And they were.

A day or two later, they found him hiding in the overhead back aft somewhere and put him in the brig for safekeeping. But the story took a sad turn one night a week later, when they called general quarters and passed the "man overboard" alert. By the time we were secured from general quarters, we learned that the marines in the brig had been giving the young seaman apprentice an exercise walk on a weather deck (an external deck open to the sea). Suddenly and without warning, the lad bolted and leapt over the side, disappearing into the darkness and the sea. He was never found. A few days later, that damn Leading Chief assigned me to the ceremony detail. It was a nice ceremony.

I can recall one other ceremony. One fine day during operations, a warrant officer, apparently looking for the wallet he had dropped, walked behind a jet while the engine was running. He was immediately blown overboard. Poor fellow, he was never found. I found myself back on the flight deck in my whites for the ceremony.

On a lighter note, I had quite the learning experience on my second cruise. I encountered the Sea Bat.

One evening after flight operations had been completed for the day, someone came into the office, and told me they had captured a Sea Bat on the flight deck.

"Nuts", I said. "There's no such thing as a Sea Bat."

"Oh yes there is, man," the sailor insisted.

"Like hell there is," I stuck to my guns.

We discussed it for another few moments and he finally persuaded me to go up on the flight deck, which was the next deck above. I went with him down the passageway, through a hatch and a short distance down a weather deck. It was an absolutely gorgeous summer evening, still light out.

I went up a short ladder and onto the flight deck. In the middle of the after flight deck was a large circle of men, standing staring, and talking. In the middle of the circle, was an upended wooden box. One man stood bent over, seeming to be peering under the box. I was motioned into the circle and advanced casually.

The man invited me to look under the box. In a moment, I found out the truth. As I bent over to lift up the box, someone stepped out of the crowd, briskly swung a broom, and caught me squarely in the seat with the head. Rudely straightened up, I couldn't decide whether to glare or laugh. All around me dozens of sailors roared and guffawed.

Don't believe anyone if they come up to you on a ship and announce they've captured a Sea Bat...

Another highlight of one of our cruises, I can't remember which, I think everyone was anticipating liberty in Australia. I personally was just about to lick my own eyebrows. And then the ridiculous happened. A typhoon. The ship's captain did the only thing he could do: brought her about like hell to lose the storm and steam for the

Philippines. But it didn't completely work. We got caught in it anyway.

...Urp. No place to get seasick!

I can still remember walking into the squadron office, just as a case of paper came flying off of one of the special safety shelves with lips that we had and catching the thing whether I wanted it or not. Of course, it wasn't all that bad, as the O Boat rode out a storm easily compared to a destroyer. Piece of cake. Except for one thing. That night, we had a ship about the size of a destroyer come alongside and we attempted to transfer fuel from her. The fuel hose broke and the next morning, after we had left the storm behind and come out to check the flight deck, there were planes everywhere, covered with avgas, a thick brown oily affair. Such a mess.

Close-up shot of the mess

Chapter 6

Fragrant Harbor

Early explorers looked upon the bay with flower blossoms floating gently on it and, breathing in the delicate scent, promptly dubbed the place "Hong Kong", Fragrant Harbor. Hundreds of years later, in 1969, oil and sewage had long since made a travesty of this poetic observation.

The large, polluted bay was now the harbor of one of the most storied cities in Asia, the Pearl of the Orient. It was a vast city, teeming with people and activity and no end of things to see and do. It was and is one of my favorite places. My memories of it are strong and warm.

The USS ORISKANY steamed slowly but steadily out of the South China Sea, along a cliff-lined shore, into Hong Kong harbor. I had been kept busy by my duties in the squadron office, located just under the flight deck, and thus wasn't able to go out to the weather deck to watch our approach. When I finally did, we were surrounded by the city, dropping anchor.

To our left, off the port beam, was the mainland side of Hong Kong, known as Kowloon. We called it "Kowloon Side". To our starboard side, was the island portion of the city, on the opposite side of which was a community called Aberdeen.

In the center of the island was an enormous mountain, Victoria Peak, which was dotted with the homes of the wealthy and traversed by a tramline, which snaked its way to the summit, where there was an observation deck, tourist spots and a very nice terraced restaurant facing the sea. The large shopping district at the foot of Victoria Peak, on the west side of the island, was called Wanchei. All day long, ferries ran between Wanchei and Kowloon carrying countless thousands of shoppers and residents.

We had dropped anchor several hundred yards off of Wanchei. I found the city absolutely amazing, and couldn't wait to go on my first liberty in this crowded, intriguing place.

On my first afternoon ashore, I marveled at the place, with its little convenience stores on seemingly every corner, selling ice cream, soda and other treats. Block after block was crowded with shops of every description, filling the air with the competing odors of hemp, tea, rice, fish, spices, onions, and garlic.

At one point, as it does in the tropics, there was a sudden squall, showering the city with warm rain. I remember taking a photo of a nearby corner for some reason in the middle of the downpour, and inadvertently captured a young couple holding hands in front of a shop. That photo is still with me, somewhere in a box, a cryptic record of a long ago moment on a rain-drenched street. I occasionally wonder where they are now, if they married or not.

One place that most sailors visited while in Hong Kong was the China Fleet Club. But the China Fleet Club was far from just a bar. It was a complete facility that boasted at least one bar, a sit-down restaurant, and a superb store selling the cameras, stereos and other goods coveted by the sailors. An amazing place.

The Mighty O at anchor in Hong Kong harbor in a shot taken from somewhere high with my new Asahi Pentax 35mm camera, now a victim of the Digital Revolution. Note the two ferries in the background. They have now been supplanted by a huge, beautiful, new bridge.

The China Fleet Club catered to a multinational crowd. I discovered this on my first visit when I encountered a contingent of British sailors in the bar, who were quite cordial. One of the sailors regaled me with stories of shipboard life on his vessel, which had a helipad on it. I cracked up helplessly as he referred to the air department on his ship as the "Airy Fairies". Later, I bought a high-quality 35mm outfit there, which I still have, although it's in need of work now, and has fallen victim to the digital revolution.

Not long after getting my camera outfit, I did something that is now habit for me: I took a city tour. Wherever you are, the best way to familiarize yourself with a city and become more comfortable in it is to take a city tour. I also took the "night" tour, which was even more memorable.

The city tour gathered and left on a pier near where launches landed from the ORISKANY. It took us all around the city. We traveled briefly through Wanchei and took a ferry across the harbor and drove through the shop-lined streets of Kowloon. I particularly remember Kings Road, famed for its shops. The neighborhood was amazingly honeycombed with myriad side streets jammed with shops. Before we turned back, we went all the way out to the border between the Hong Kong Colony and China. It was in the middle of nondescript farmland, not much to look at.

Once we reached the harbor, we took another ferry back and drove around the crowded district of Wanchei, and went around to the east side of the island to the community called Aberdeen. Aberdeen has an enclosed harbor, with a large, colorfully painted restaurant floating in the center of it. Not too originally, it was called the Floating Seafood Restaurant and was popular tourist spot. Probably still is. We had to take little water taxies shaped like small junks out to it

I can still remember the picturesque stairway inside the front door, which led upstairs to the restaurant. The wall along it was covered over with the autographed photos of movie stars who had visited there in the past. William Holden, who had done a couple of films there around 1960, smiled out of one photo.

The restaurant lived up to its name and precious little non-seafood was served there, which was a problem for me as I just couldn't cope with seafood. But I managed to get by.

After lunch, we drove back around the island, ending the tour by taking a tram up to the summit of Victoria Peak. The view was breathtaking. We could see for miles. In the mid distance we could see the ORISKANY's huge hulk anchored in the harbor. We could see it all. It was an amazing experience for a young man to stand on a mountain top with a city spread before him in the evening like diamonds on black velvet.

On the other side of the summit was a small, terraced restaurant on the hillside. From there, we could look out to sea in the fading light. I remember that my shipmates and I, before returning to the ship, had dinner at the little restaurant on an outdoor terrace which was softly lit by small lanterns mounted on posts.

Later in our stay, we took the night tour during which there was a visit to a Chinese-style nightclub, followed by much rumbling through the narrow streets of the city in a tour bus. I have a dim memory of getting there by a small boat from Wanchei which moored near the club and then we walked down a narrow walkway to the back door of the club. It was neat inside with ornate little lamps on each table little the faces of guest eerily from below.

Traditional entertainment in a nightclub on Kowloon side

During the 1970 cruise, an incident happened aboard ship that I still find inexplicable. One evening when I was the Duty Yeoman, I was summoned to Sick Bay to "write up" a third class petty officer in our squadron. "Writing up" someone was essentially putting them on report.

When I got there, he was strapped onto an exam table, groaning loudly, his eyes rolling wildly, his face bruised and puffy. I could tell he had been through a rough ride. He looked all too unfortunately like the Pillsbury Doughboy. As I took notes, someone described the incident. I couldn't believe it.

The man in question, Bill Darrin (not his real name), was being helped to his rack by a shipmate after he had injured his leg on liberty. To get to the VF-194 berthing area, they had to go through a large compartment amidships, which housed a contingent of U.S. Marines. We usually called it the "Marine Compartment" for short.

Halfway through the compartment, Darrin and his shipmate came abreast of a marine sentry, at parade rest holding a baton in front him with two hands. (I had seen the sentries and they were impressive). Suddenly Darrin gave the marine a lightning kick in the crotch. The poor man doubled forward immediately.

To straighten him up, Darrin then gave the hapless marine a knee in the face. Unfortunately for Darrin, there were several marines nearby who were far from pleased by his performance. Before things had been brought under control a few minutes later, the marines had exacted their vengeance on Darrin, hugely reformatting him with their fists.

Darrin lost his petty officer's "crow" in the ensuing Captain's Mast, although his sudden outburst of violence was never clearly explained. He was evidently given to senseless behavior when he had been drinking. Heaven knows what's happened to him since, although I wish him well.

After electronics, the next most popular thing for sailors to buy in Hong Kong was clothes. And, indeed, Hong Kong is famous for its tailors. However, buying clothes there was a tricky affair, as there were tailors and there were tailors.

I remember that the navy put out detailed tips to sailors about the many facets of liberty in Hong Kong, which definitely included warnings about tailors. For example, a favorite technique of the shady tailors was to offer sailors alcoholic drinks during fittings. Later, when the sailor showed up to pick up his clothes, he had no clear memory of how the fitting had gone. Many a seaman opened a package of tailored clothes at sea, on the way back home to the states, and discovered they were the proud owners of a bunch of really badly fitting garments.

I was luckier than the average, as my new suits fit reasonably well. There were also about half a dozen monogrammed shirts that lasted many years. Then summer after I returned, I wore one of my suits, the light brown pinstripe, and it help land me the job I stayed with for over thirty–one years.   But the plain-toed tan oxfords that I had made at another shop were just too damned small. Whoever made them didn't allow for any spare room beyond my actual foot size.   They looked neat, and I was occasionally mistaken for an officer, but they were torture to wear.

Well, you live and you learn.

Chapter 7

Sasebo Nights

Sasebo was an orderly port with pleasant, green hills rising gently around the deep blue harbor, a peaceful place. The scenery reminded me, and still does, of the picturesque backgrounds in old Japanese monster movies.

As a military port, Sasebo was founded in 1886, becoming a major facility for the Japanese navy during the First Sino-Japanese War, the Russo-Japanese War, and World War II. Following World War II, a part of the base was taken over by the United States Navy and named U.S. Fleet Activities Sasebo. The rest of the harbor was and is shared with the Japan Maritime Self-Defense Force.

It was my first taste of Japan, and a fascinating one. I marveled, and still do, at the incredible order and tidiness of the place, the shops filled with a plentitude of consumer goods, the bustling crowds on the streets. Another major place of interest for sailors on our ship was a district nicknamed Sailor Town, not far from the waterfront. By night it was an almost magical place with its colorful neon signs illuminating the doors of countless tiny clubs along twisting, narrow streets. If a sailor wasn't in the mood for a club, there were the "stand bars", places where there was no seating, but a long counter to belly up to, where one could just have a beer or bite to eat without having to contend with B-girls.

A Sasebo stand bar

Another view of Sailor Town

During the days we were there, I roamed about Sailor Town and the business district, having a hard time with the language barrier. Once, I tried to find some racy reading in a bookstore. There wasn't a single book there in English. My God, complete no-go, all in Japanese. I still have no idea at all what they read.

On one outing, I went to a shop that specialized in customized stuff such as baseball caps and mugs. I ordered a mug that was beautifully finished in a day with a picture of Dennis the Menace on one side (that was a nickname I had picked up due to my being short, blond and resembling Dennis, and "Yeoman Bowman" on the other side. It was a treasured possession until it got broken accidentally in the hangar at Miramar few months later. It wasn't until over ten years later that a shipmate of mine in the reserves who was a draftsman come up with new artwork and then I ordered replacement mug which I have to this day on my mantelpiece.

A large covered mall area in Sasebo, looking very futuristic

Another thing I found out in a hurry—when in Japan, at least during that era, ordering a glass of milk in a restaurant did not get you what you expected if you were a Westerner. They brought you a glass of hot milk sweetened with sugar. It was sweetened because the milk in question was canned, frequently tasted funny, and that's apparently how they made it more palatable. It was last time I ordered a glass of milk in a restaurant overseas.

After all these years, an interesting experience on one of our visits to Sasebo still stands out in my mind. In the evening, I went to the enlisted men's club there, which was located on a low hilltop, along with a shipmate who was an aviation storekeeper, AK Lopez (not his real name). During the cruise, I had become a close friend of Lopez, as well as another sailor of Hispanic descent, finally almost becoming an honorary Hispanic myself. For a while, it seemed that every week they taught me one or two obscene words in Spanish.

We were sitting in the Acey-Ducey bar (for first and second class petty officers) having a beer when a young lad, a seaman, who couldn't have been more than seventeen, approached Lopez and me. He leaned forward and asked me if I would go to the Package Store and buy him a bottle of booze. For those, who don't know, package stores, which sell liquor by the bottle, don't sell to anyone under 21, or who are not a petty officer. They make you sign for the bottles, which have serial numbers on them.

I immediately declined the young fellow's request. Having repeatedly heard the navy's warnings against buying booze in bottles for under-aged sailors, I did not want to sample the fare at the brig.

"Bowman", Lopez muttered disgustedly in his Spanish accent, "I'm not afraid—I'll do it!" He got up and left with the young man.

The next day, both Lopez and I had the duty, and we happened to meet in the hangar bay back aft. Lopez looked shaken.

"I've learned my lesson," Lopez said with conviction, "I'll never do that again. Last night that kid who I bought the liquor for got in trouble and was picked up by the Shore Patrol. The only reason I didn't get in trouble was that he poured the booze into another bottle with a different serial number." He rolled his eyes in relief.

I couldn't suppress a soft chuckle. Wearing a petty officer's crow carries responsibility with it.

The last day of our visit in Sasebo in the summer of 1969 was close. It was after one of those "lost nights" that sailors still have. I awoke a little later than I should have in her apartment and had to hurry to get cleaned up, dressed and call a cab. After a relatively short trip across town, during which I was very tense, the cab slid up to the pier where the ship was moored, with little more than twenty minutes to spare before the end of liberty. The one thing sailors never want to do is to get back to the ship late after the end of liberty. It's called "Missing Ship's Movement" and invariably provokes some sort of discipline, although it's understandable, as it's disruptive and expensive for the navy to be shipping sailors everywhere to catch up with their ships. A few years before that I had gotten back late from liberty in Seattle and found out firsthand it about. I was lucky and drew an XO's mast, which was unofficial and was restricted to the ship for the remainder of the two week cruise.

Gratefully, I hustled up the after brow, saluted the Petty Officer of the Watch, and made my way to the squadron office under the flight deck. The leading chief, nursing a fierce hangover, was presiding over the debarkation procedures, including accounting for all hands in his paperwork.

Shortly after that we cast off and steamed for Yankee Station.

Chapter 8

The Hand of God

It was just another quiet, routine day, December 22, 1969, shortly after I had returned from my first cruise. We were based at NAS Miramar, located some fifteen miles north of San Diego. It was a pleasant base, well laid out and lined with picturesque palm trees. I was absolutely thunderstruck a few years ago when I learned that it had been converted to a Marine Corps Air Station. And it was not just because it had gone to the Marine Corps. That was merely a touch of the strange and melancholy. Back in the 80s, Hollywood had shot part of the now legendary film *Top Gun* there, immortalizing "Fighter Town USA", as it was known, as the quintessential naval air base. But I knew that in the intervening years, the government had allowed developers to build houses and apartments pretty much to the edge of the base, which was recipe for disaster to me. And, indeed, in recent years there have been a crash or two there, which has cast a pall over the\future of MCAS Miramar.

Broadway Fountain in Horton plaza,
in downtown San Diego. The plaza has long
since been remodeled but the fountain, installed
in 1870, and a centerpiece of every sailor's
liberty, remains as a beloved landmark

I sat tapping with no great ardor on my typewriter in the squadron office, at work on some paperwork that I have long forgotten since that startling morning. The office was located along one wall of the hangar, with the rest of the floor space taken up with maintenance area for jets and another wall of offices on the other side. We shared the large structure with at least one other unit, maybe two.

Very unexpectedly, there was a thunderous noise and the building shook violently. "Oh my God," I thought. "Some idiot out in the hangar must have dropped some ordnance while trying to load it on a jet. Oh my God—"

Jumping to my feet, I dashed out into the passageway, where there were a series of elongated windows which looked out into the hangar's interior. I was confronted with a nightmarish scene straight out of Dante's Inferno. The hangar was an insane jumble of flaming jets and chaos. The next thing I knew the emergency alarms were going off and we were all sprinting down the long passageway for the front door.

"Don't panic!" someone shouted as we ran. We were too busy trying to get the hell out of the building to think about much else. Outside, fire-fighting teams formed and began running hoses in to the hangar to put out the blaze. I found myself on one of them, but my end of the hose never got past the hangar doors. It was just as well, as I later heard that those at the front of the hose encountered unforgettable horrors as they reached injured, dying or dead shipmates in those first few minutes.

An almost bigger concern at the time was the system of concrete drainage channels under the hangar. It fed under other adjacent hangars and there was a very real danger that flaming oil could seep through under them and burn down everything. We worked intensively for the better part of an hour before things were under control.

It wouldn't be until later that day that I would get details, but for now, I only knew that there had been a crash. A jet had plowed through the front doors of the hangar at fairly high speed. The result had been terrifying, destructive, and deadly.

I remember being sent to the barracks area for lunch, and as I walked the half a mile or so to the barracks and mess hall, I could see a grim reminder of the crash, a dark oblong in the hangar roof. Immediately, I knew that only one thing could have made the hole: the detonated ejection seat of a jet fighter.

That afternoon after lunch, back in the squadron office, I was put to work on special paperwork to deal with the crash. The officer who had been at the controls of the jet stood nearby, in blank-faced shock. I felt for him. It had been a routine training flight that had gone awry when the jet's hydraulics went out, leaving the pilot with little control. Following procedure, the pilot had pointed the aircraft toward the open desert that used to surround NAS Miramar and ejected.

Then fate took over as the hydraulics unexpectedly kicked back in and the jet banked back toward the row of hangars on the airstrip. I was later told that originally the F8J Crusader was heading right for the portion of the hangar where I was sitting. But the hand of God intervened and the runaway jet changed course again, finally slamming into the middle of the hangar doors at about 250 miles an hour. Overall, 22 people were lost that day, only one of them from my unit, VF-194, a senior chief. But for the hand of God, it would have been two or even more.

I remember that still later that afternoon I had something to do with base legal. Investigators had decided that an ADJ3 (Aviation Machinist Mate 3rd Class) had not inspected an oil seal which later caused the jet's engine to fail sometime after takeoff. He was in our office for a while and then was taken away, reportedly to face a general court-martial. I never saw him again, although I have often wondered whether he was convicted and what happened to him. Nor would I ever again see the officer who had been piloting the jet, ironically the Personnel Officer. He was immediately given a transfer to another unit. It was understandable, probably standard procedure. You couldn't blame the navy there.

Somewhere in my navy papers, I have a padded presentation folder containing a certificate of commendation I received from the base commanding officer. It was for helping on a fire-fighting team after the crash, a melancholy reminder of a long-ago disaster.

The next day I was off on Christmas leave and things got better. A bright New Year, my second cruise to Westpac and the end of my active duty lay just ahead.

Chapter 9

City Of Madame Butterfly

To this day, it is not clear what the truth is, but for one reason or another, the legendary city of Nagasaki has been associated with the beloved Puccini opera Madame Butterfly, ever since the opera premiered over a century ago in Milan, Italy. It is known that in 1922, eighteen years after the premiere of the opera, noted Japanese singer Miura Tamaki, famous for her portrayal of Madame Butterfly, visited wealthy Scottish businessman Thomas Glover in Nagasaki. For many years it was said that Glover met and married the daughter of a local samurai. Glover's bride was said to habitually wear kimonos emblazoned with butterflies. However, in recent years, this story has been called into question, but it is still strongly felt that events that formed the basis of the opera occurred in Nagasaki in the early 1890s.

Whatever the truth, Nagasaki is a magical and beautiful city, long a major southwestern port of Japan. During one of our visits to Sasebo in the middle of the first cruise, I remember going on another of those tours arranged by the ship's chaplain. God bless that chap wherever he may be. That was the most memorable outing I went on in Westpac.

We boarded a bus on the pier and set out across the island of Kyushu for Nagasaki, site of one the atomic bomb attacks near the end of World War II. The scenery was remarkable. As the bus traversed the Japanese countryside, we passed all sorts of colorful farm buildings, as well as picturesque temples perched on hillsides. Most of them were undoubtedly centuries old. Also, from time to time, there would be in the distance an ancient cemetery. All about the countryside there was an aura of peace, order, and dignity.

Nagasaki turned out to be located along a deep blue bay, opposite enormous Mt. Inasa, the top of which could reached by a sky tram from the other side of the harbor. During our stay, which lasted two to three days, we had amazing adventures.

On our first day there, we rode the sky tram to the summit of the peak and were in awe at the sweeping view. We also knocked around the quiet neighborhood surrounding our traditional Japanese-style hotel occasionally coming across beautiful wooden temples perched on the steep hillside. I can still remember marveling at the peaceful afternoon in that neighborhood and how I was able to quietly roam around a place that my country had once catastrophically attacked.

The hotel itself was a learning experience. I shared a room with another sailor, and looking out the window, we could see the rooftops of Nagasaki. This was an enchanting sight on a misty morning, which I still fondly remember. It took some time to get used to the Japanese-style toilet in the bathroom, which was little more than an indentation in the floor, although the traditional Japanese bathtub was easier to take. You walked up a few steps and then stepped down into it, to sit in water up to your neck. It was remarkably soothing.

What a memorable place. But there was some trepidation regarding wearing uniforms. That was because even in 1970, the navy was still concerned about hard feelings toward the U.S. military over the 1945 bombing. Also, it was August, the anniversary month of the attack. As it turned out, there were no problems, and I was able to move about unnoticed.

In the center of the city was a large park, built over what had once been ground zero when the bomb had hit. It was the most peaceful place I've ever been. In some places, grass still did not grow twenty-five years later. There was an extensive museum built on a nearby hill overlooking ground zero, filled with panoramic photos taken after the bomb was dropped. It was a special experience visit to Nagasaki indeed, on the 25th anniversary of the attack.

Below is an image of a fragment of building that I am sure still stands there today.

A building on "ground zero" in Nagasaki

To the north was another large park, the Peace Park. It was dedicated to the hope that such an atomic attack would never again happen to Nagasaki. A huge complex, it contained an enormous stone statue of Peace, its arms outstretched in placation, as well as a large fountain and extensive grounds to allow visitors to walk and contemplate the folly of war.

While I was at the park, a shipmate took a photo of me standing in front of the statue of Peace staring up at it. I later used it in the squadron newsletter, which I edited. Somewhere in my things, I still have an 8x10 of that picture. It is a fond reminder of that long-ago visit to Nagasaki. It is reproduced below.

One thing I noticed early on in Japan is that, at least back then, their beer bottles were by U.S. standards humongous, something around a quart. There was no way you could or even would want to drink a six pack! Heck, I can't remember whether I was able to even finish a single bottle. Pop, on the other hand, came in extremely thin cans that looked exactly like current energy drink cans. It gave one the feeling they liked their beer a lot more than their soda in Japan.

Chapter 10

Spook Deck

September 1970. We were steaming through a gray dusk near Korea, apparently as part of some maneuver. I had been running around the flight deck, as was my practice, for exercise, having gotten off work for the day. It was good to get outside for a while and get away from the cramped confines of the little squadron office.

Looking around, I noticed that our escort (destroyers, cruisers, etc.) were all black silhouettes, lit only by an occasional blinking colored light. Momentarily, I was puzzled, but it was time for me to go below for dinner, so I started toward a hatch. I soon realized along the way that the entire carrier task force was in the middle of a blackout exercise.

A blackout exercise is a combat training evolution, in which every bit of white light aboard a ship that's visible from the outside is extinguished. The only visible lights allowed are colored—red, green, blue. That's because they can't be seen for much of any distance by a potential enemy. Blackout exercises are more than a bit eerie.

I had to go down the equivalent of three decks to reach the hangar bay. The whole way was pitch black, a real safety violation, I told myself. There wasn't a single colored safety light. I slowly inched my way through dark passageways, stopping for a short while in the squadron office, which was lit by white light. For a short while, a Filipino shipmate, inspired by the blackout exercise, regaled me with eerie ghost tales of his homeland. Thanks, friend, I thought, just what I needed. I left the office, continuing down the passageway, across what was essentially a footbridge with cables for railings. Some eighteen to twenty feet below was the hangar bay. Going down several ladders, I reached the hangar deck, stepped through a hatch and went down two more decks, to what we called the "main deck". There, at least, were safety lights, blood red, which were mounted near the deck every fifteen or twenty feet.

Able to see better now, I made my way a little more quickly. I moved past the place near the Marine spaces, where Darrin had his lightning karate moment with the marine sentry before being turned into a medical case. Continuing, I moved toward a t-intersection in the passageway. To the left and around the corner was the large, double-wide ladder going down to the mess decks.

As I reached the intersection, there was suddenly a tall, cadaverous figure standing there, dressed in dungarees and Dixie cup cap. His arms hung loosely at his sides and his eyes were wide open, staring, and all whites. He stood wordlessly for just a moment and then was gone.

I stopped in the red gloom in astonishment. Looking about me, I could see nobody. The passageway was deserted. What was going on here? Reaching a decision, I did something that I don't think I would do now, being

72

older and theoretically wiser. I followed the figure I had seen.

I decided that the sailor had gone down the hatch in the deck to my left, which led to berthing areas. The second deck down was where I had slept on the previous cruise. Quickly, I scrambled down the ladder.

But there were only men sleeping on bunks, red night-lights, the distant whine of engines below. I immediately went down the ladder to the next deck, encountering exactly the same tableau: a berthing compartment full of sleeping sailors, dimly lit by red night-lights.

It was then that I suddenly asked myself why I was chasing a phantasm in a blackout exercise. Not having any reasonable answer for myself, I shot straight up the two ladders. Emerging, I headed around the corner and down the double-wide ladder to the mess decks, where there were white lights, food, people talking.

After over forty years, I'm still not sure of what I saw.

Chapter 11

DaNang Dog Days

As the summer of 1970 drew to a close, so did the term of my active duty. I learned that I would be sent home in mid-September for separation. Although I had had many happy times on the O-Boat, I was anxious to be return home to the rainforest greenery of Western Washington and my normal life.

A few days before I was due to be flown off the ship, I had a minor adventure which I still remember vividly. During the course of my duties, I had to traverse the main passageway outside the squadron office. It ran the entire length of the ship and was segmented at about 25 foot intervals by steel walls with oval openings and hatches. Seagoing types call these combings.

To speed things up, I would trot along, hopping through each open hatch, or combing. After all, I had to go half the length of the ship to get to the admiral's office for paperwork. Designated CAG (Carrier Air Group), the admiral commanded all the jet squadrons stationed on our ship.

Most openings had high enough tops that there was no problem. But a few, a scant few, were low. That fateful day, I didn't notice the low hatch opening and jumped high.

A moment later, I was flat on my back, with a humongous headache, struggling to remember who I was and where I was. I had quite literally knocked myself silly. Swiveling my head to my left, I was able to stare straight through an open hatch and into a compartment, where several men sat unconcernedly playing cards. I lay there for several minutes, but nobody seemed to notice.

I don't think they ever knew I was there on the deck, outside their compartment. Staggering to my feet, I put my hand to the top of my head and felt something wet. It was blood. A few minutes later, I made it to sickbay, where they promptly put three stitches in me and sent me on my way.

Three days later, I walked through the ORISKANY for the last time with my luggage. For some reason, I had thought I would be flown off the ship in a COD (Carrier Onboard Delivery, a large prop plane), but instead, I was trundled aboard a large helicopter with several other short-timers.

Inside the giant aircraft, it was completely empty, except for a long bench along the starboard bulkhead, where we all sat down and buckled ourselves in for safety. A short while later, the huge machine lifted up from the flight deck of the aircraft carrier and roared slowly across the water towards the Vietnamese mainland. The noise it made was unbelievable. I have never forgotten it.

The flight was not long, ending after about twenty minutes or so at the sizeable airfield near DaNang. There, they loaded us into a truck and carted us to what was apparently the Naval Support Activity DaNang, a couple of miles away. I was surprised at the whole area. Rather than being a large coherent affair, DaNang was a collection of military compounds and clusters of civilian houses. At one point, I could see a distant stretch of apparently store-type buildings near some water. Probably, that was what was once downtown DaNang.

At the height of the American involvement in Vietnam, the port of DaNang, South Vietnam, was the Navy's largest overseas shore command. From this port city, over 200,000 U.S., Vietnamese, and allied forces fighting in the I Corps Tactical Zone were supplied with everything that they needed to combat the VC and NVA aggressors.

The U.S. Navy established the MST-1 detachment to train Vietnamese crews and maintain PTFs in February 1964. The PTFs, under Vietnamese officers and crews, conducted over 1,000 raids against North Vietnam from March-April 1964 to January 1972. Because of DaNang's strategic location on rail, air, and highway routes, development of its facilities into a large deepwater port was essential. By the end of 1964, preparations were well underway to improve DaNang's base and port facilities. The airfield was expanded and new runways were constructed, so were piers, fuel farms, warehouses, and ammunition magazines. Marine ground security and helicopter units were stationed at the airfield.

When Marines deployed to Vietnam in large numbers beginning in March 1965, DaNang became the focus of the growing War. For the next four years, DaNang hosted various Army Divisions, and two Marine Divisions of the III Marine Amphibious Force. Together these forces, along with allied and South Vietnamese units, fought the VC and NVA enemy in the I Corps Tactical Zone. The Navy provided logistics support to the Coastal Surveillance Forces that patrolled offshore to interdict the smuggling of arms and supplies by North Vietnam to the South by sea. The PBRs of Task Force CLEARWATER fought to keep the rivers of I Corps open to allied logistics traffic. The

DaNang base became home to the Seabee's 13th Naval Construction Regiment, and – later – the 3rd Naval Construction Brigade and 32nd Naval Construction Regiment.

DaNang reached its peak in 1969. At that time the command controlled 250 ships, landing craft, lighters, tugs, barges, floating cranes that made it the largest concentration of such vessels in all of Southeast Asia. The command had 450 officers, 10,000 sailors, and had a civilian work force of 11,000 Vietnamese and civilian contractors. There were three deep-draft ship piers for ocean-going ships, while LSTs used the Tien Sha, Bridge, Museum, and Ferry cargo facilities. The port controlled 900,000 square feet of supply depot space, 2.7 million square feet of open-air storage space, and 500,000 cubic feet of refrigerated storage space. The port handled 320,000 tons of cargo.

The compound at the support activity was also surprising to me. The media had given me the impression that life was grubby and gritty in Vietnam. But the compound was a large, tidy group of buildings with packed dirt roads between them. Everything was neat and chipper. All around the place marched people in crisply starched fatigues. You might almost have mistaken the compound for a facility stateside, if it wasn't for the lack of pavement, the distant crackle of a firefight, the stuttering of circling choppers, the wisps of gun smoke drifting up from the jungle.

For the three days we were in DaNang, we stayed in neat barracks with concrete floors. I immediately noticed that bathrooms and showers were in a separate building behind the barracks, which was reached by short narrow path.

The next morning, I found out why the bathrooms and showers were in a separate building: their moisture was compellingly attractive to bugs, big bugs. As I walked through the front door of the building, a roach passed me that was so enormous that I almost said "good morning" to it. I didn't make a move to harm it. What the hell. It left the building promptly and without bothering me and I do not have much of any killer instinct. Live and let live. For the rest of my stay in DaNang, I hardly saw another bug.

During the stay in DaNang, there was little for us to do, really. Between meals, we were free, with mostly reading, sleeping or going to the base movie to occupy us. I remember one hot afternoon sitting in base theater, a facility so informal that it didn't even have a door. They were showing *Zig Zag,* a thriller with George Kennedy. It's funny what you can remember after thirty-five years. The heat apparently made a number of us drowsy, including me. I slept through most of it.

Late on the third day, they loaded us in the trailer of a semi, with the back open. Back then, this sort of transport was used a lot, both overseas and in bases on the states, crude but effective.

It was raining moderately heavily as the truck left the navy compound and drove at about twenty-five miles per hour towards the airfield. I squatted near the open back doors and watched as rows of crude little houses went by, a single lit light bulb hanging in the living room of each. Occasionally, someone would stare out of a window at our truck, or stand staring at us in front their home. It was a melancholy affair, which still haunts me a little. Those were people who were beat down by war, weary, uncertain, short of hope. And we were leaving them in their war torn little half acre.

A short while later we were on a chartered Boeing airliner flying east for home. Eventually, after a six hour layover on Guam, due to engine trouble, and a total transit time of about twenty-four hours, we reached Travis Air Force Base outside of San Francisco.

There was a bus ride to the San Francisco airport, another flight, and I reached San Diego, where I spent a week or so at Naval Station San Diego. Eventually, thank God, the processing was over and I was separated from active duty. I wasted no time in getting to the airport and taking my flight to Seattle.

I made it back home. But now, more than forty years have slipped by, bringing joy, pain, love, achievement, failure, travel, and friends. A civilian career started and eventually ended, long, satisfying and full of experiences. My time in the naval reserve also ended after twenty-five years of service. One day in 1991, I shook hands with a couple of officers in the VTU (Voluntary Training Unit) that was my last assignment, and mustered out with a golden crow and an armload of gold hash marks.

But Westpac isn't completely gone now. For, whenever I'm near a navy ship and smell creosote, fuel oil, the tang of the sea air, and hear seagulls squawk, the memories come back. Memories of Westpac.

Epilogue

On Halloween 1992, a local television station in Seattle aired a magazine program, which profiled the USS ORISKANY. I was sitting in my living room with my late beloved, watching TV that night, when the show came on. It was a surprising and spooky confirmation of my own experience years before in the blackout exercise off of Korea.

The Mighty O-Boat, in mothballs for many years, had become the ghost boat of Bremerton Naval Shipyard, across the sound from Seattle. According to the program, the ORISKANY had been undergoing salvage operations for some time, preparatory to being scrapped. Salvaging refers to removing about everything that can be removed from a ship: gadgets from bulkheads, speakers, lamps, bells, brass portholes, nameplates, you name it.

The shipyard employees hated to work on the ORISKANY, of all the ships in the yard. Tools floated, they said. Hatches opened and closed by themselves. Employees also reported that they occasionally walked into ghostly apparitions unexpectedly in passageways. Perhaps strangest of all, employees reported smelling food cooking in the mess deck. No food had been cooked there since shortly after the end of the Vietnam War.

The program discussed the disastrous fire of 1966 aboard the ORISKANY, which burned through the mess deck and officers' quarters, claiming 34 lives, and speculated whether the restless souls of the victims might still be walking the decks of the huge empty vessel. One thing was certain, the program concluded: most of the disturbances onboard the old 1940s vintage aircraft carrier centered around the mess deck. That was in the area where I had my own encounter on that long-ago night.

It made it a better than average possibility that whatever I had encountered in the blood red gloom of that long-ago blackout exercise was something not of mundane normality.

I made a video recording of the program that I have to this day.

In the spring of 1995, a Seattle newspaper featured a front-page article reporting the movement of the USS ORISKANY from Bremerton Naval Shipyard to another location for scrapping. There was a beautiful color photo of the O-Boat being slowly towed out into Puget Sound.

The years passed and somewhere around 2002, I did some research on the Internet into the fate of the ORISKANY. Along the way, I found a couple of sites run by and dedicated to former crewmembers of the ORISKANY. They brought back many warm and poignant memories.

I was surprised to find on one site a photo of the huge hulk of the ORISKANY riding at anchor off the coast of

Galveston, Texas. According to the write-up, the O-Boat was still awaiting scrapping.

Still awaiting scrapping? Seven years after leaving Bremerton? I was a bit surprised and puzzled. Could it be that the ORISKANY was just as unnerving a vessel to the scrappers as it was to the salvagers?

In the winter of 2006, I did some more Internet research on the O-Boat. I was a bit surprised to learn that the ORISKANY was now scheduled to be reefed. It seemed a fitting end for her, and I liked the idea. There was no definite date given at that time, although the article inferred that it might not happen for a while.

A few months later, I happened to check the net and discovered a date had been set for the reefing the following week. It made sense. The hurricane season was approaching and there was no way they could properly and safely sink the O-Boat in a storm.

The article made another revelation that may explain the long, eleven year delay that had passed without the ship being scrapped. According to the article, the corporation which had bid on scrapping the vessel had defaulted on its contract. Was this also confirmation that the scrappers just didn't want to work on the old ship?

On Wednesday, May 17, 2006, the USS ORISKANY was towed to a location 24 miles off the coast of Pensacola, Florida and sunk in 220 feet of water, where she will slowly metamorphose into an artificial reef. I saw no mention of her reefing that day, but the next day there were articles, video and pictures on the net.

It had seemed like a good idea up until then. But as I sat looking at the photos on the computer screen of the old ship shuddering down into the warm, caressing, blue water, stern first, I couldn't help feeling a brief moment of sadness.

The O-Boat went down in 37 minutes, they later said. It was perfectly executed, complete with explosive charges detonated below the water line. It was done at just the right moment, to ensure that she went down quickly and cleanly, so that debris and possible oil seepage would be minimal. A couple of ships were kept nearby for a few days to clean up anything that surfaced.

The Mighty O now rests in the deep, her long odyssey finally over, her service finished. Her decks are stilled, the planes and personnel all gone, her compartments flooded and dark. Her days of cruising the Tonkin Gulf are done, but she is not merely a vast inert hulk. She lives on in the hearts and minds of those who served aboard her, steeped in over fifty years of memories, emotions, ghosts. And I find myself wondering if the restless shades of those lost long ago in the fire of 19661967 still move noiselessly through her submerged, lightless passageways, searching for the way out, for peace. Hopefully, they have found it by now.

Rest in Peace.

\

Squadron Newsletter Reproductions

What follows are reproductions of a few issues of THE RED
LIGHTNING ILLUSTRATED.

Please note that through the wonder of modern technology, I
have been able to not only scan them but enhance them as well,
and they look better than they did originally!

--Dave

August 1969

With the end of the third line period we've finally passed "over the hump" and at last have fewer days left of the cruise than we've spent out here already. This has definitely been our best line period yet as far as meeting our assigned commitments and making up sorties for the Feedbags when they didn't have birds available. A sincere well done is in order for all hands in the maintenance department for this splendid performance—all of us Red Flash pilots are true snivelers at heart, always trying to snivel extra hops and nothing is more gratifying than to take sorties away from VF-191 day after day due to our superior maintenance. Our sincere thanks to all of you in maintenance for making it a fine line period and please keep up the good work.

Two suggestion boxes have been placed in our squadron area recently, one in air frames/power plants and one in maintenance control. Any constructive suggestions, signed or anonymous, on any facet of squadron operations both at sea and in port will be welcomed. All suggestions are seen by the CO and XO and given careful consideration. Here's your chance to see that your own ideas on how to improve the squadron are seen by the people who can do the most to see it acted upon.

One more point that did come up during the last line period is the matter of showing up in time for an integrity watch. The time to relieve the watch is 15 minutes before the hour, just like all Navy watches and of course, there is no excuse for being late to relieve a watch. All integrity watch standers should report to flight deck control at the time of relieveing for instructions from the integrity watch officer, and the POW. If anybody is late, it means a man from the off going squadron or duty is late getting relieved and it really makes the squadron look bad. The POW should contact each watch stander half an hour prior to the time of relieving and assure that he is aware of his watch. Any discrepancies should be reported to the IWO immediately. And watches take precedence over working parties - any conflicts here should be worked out in advance with the duty section leader or leading chief.

If this issue of the "Red Lightning Illustrated" goes to press as scheduled, we should be just about arriving in Hong Kong when it hits the newstands. This is of course what we've all be looking forward to for months now, a real liberty port. Many of us have never been there before and are anticipating some real good times on liberty. So, let's all get on with it and play as hard as we've worked, stay out of trouble and come back for two or three more quick line periods, pump out even more sorties than we have before, and head back to the states with a cruise we can really be proud of behind us. We've got a tremendous amount of momentum going now, let's keep it that way.

1

"WELL DONE!"

Recently, in Ready Room Five, Aboard USS ORISKANY (CVA-34) thirty four Red Flashes were honored for their services in Fighter Squadron ONE NINETY FOUR during the 1969 WestPac Cruise.

At 0900, in the morning, the Commanding Officer, CDR Joseph Vinti presented Letters of Commendation to the deserving squadron members who stepped forward to the podium one by one to accept their awards and CDR Vinti's congratulations.

The top performers of the squadron were:

ADJC Melvin DIAMOND	AME2 J. W. SALTER
AEC H. E. DAVIS	AZ2 Andy RONQUILIO
ADCS J. M. GERRITSEN	ATR3 M. A. WESSELY
PRC R. J. THOMAS	AMH3 R. S. TALBOTT
AMH1 H. R. JEFFERS	ATN3 S. P. SENSNEY
AMS1 Virgil GUY	ADJ3 SHAWN QUINN
ADJ1 Cliff HEAD	ADJ3 J. R. SECREST
AO1 H. R. HOLTZER	AMS3 G. F. PLATH
AO1 R. L. GARLICK	ADJAN M. J. WHITE
AE1 F. W. KURZINGER	ADJAN W. R. KEMP
PN2 W. A. GARRETT	AQBAN F. W. IHRKE
AE2 Charles LIGHTFOOTE	ATNAN R. R. PEACOCK
ADJ2 L. W. GILBERTSON	ADJAN Chuck QUALE
AO2 T. A. KAIKOWSKI	AMSAN T. D. DOYLE
AQF2 Tony FORTEZ	AN B. L. HARDEE
ADJ2 Gale SETFORD	

2

CHANGE OF COMMAND

Probably the most newworthy occasion of our last month was the turning over of command of the Legendary Red Lightnings by CDR Robbie ROBERTS to CDR Joe VINTI. The Red Flash Command at Sea Pin, which has been passed down through about four skippers was transferred to CDR VINTI'S chest on 9 July 1969 aboard the ORISKANY while tied up at Subic Bay.

Although the heat humidity in hangar bay one were as usual—almost unbearable—all hands held up well during the ceremony. A fine performance by the VF-194 Color Guard made the occasion especially impressive. Well done to those stalwart five, WEATHERSPEE, MUNZ, HOFSTETTER, WILSON, and SAMANIE. And of course our appreciation to the Marine Detachment for helping to train them.

In addition to our new skipper, we also got a new XO, CDR Jim RYAN, who reported aboard three days before the change of command direct from VF-124. CDR RYAN hails from Billings, Montana. He attended Montana State University and East Montana College of Education and entered the Navy in March, 1954. His previous tours of duty have included Naval War College, Demon and Phantom

3

VF-194 CHANGE OF COMMAND

4

Fighter Squadrons and duty with RCVW-12 at Miramar. His wife's name is Marjorie Jean and he has three children, Patricia, Michelle and Michael.

Following the Change of Command itself, there was a reception at the Cubi Officers' Club during which CDR ROBERTS was presented with several gifts, one of which was a silver punch bowl with tray and cups. On each cup was engraved the name of one of the officers in the squadron. A well done is in order for LT Mike O'BAR for bringing this monster safely back from Tokyo.

Later in the evening, Captain KENYON rose to an impromptu challenge raised to him and strapped himself into Red Horse One down in the Catapult Room, managing to catch the number one wire on his third attempt. He was followed by CDR DONNELLY, the Feedbags' skipper, who tried 5 times before he gave up. Our new CO, CDR VINTI then stepped in and caught the wire on his 5th attempt, thus becoming the first CVW-19 CO to enter the Red Horse Hall of Fame.

5

Animal Talk

In starting our column for this month, we must apologize for not having written an article for last month's newsletter. We suppose the liberty just got the best of us for the month of July.

It seems that finally after three months of waiting, our "Line Shack" has gotten its air conditioner running. We must admit it's not a professional installation but it does work! The last line period went very well for us, as well as the rest of the squadron due to the aircraft readiness and availability.

We also has a squadron award ceremony and the line was well represented by having 15 men recieve letters of commendation from our commanding officer. Recieving awards were Chief Thomas, Ken Keber, Dale Setford, Lee Gilbertson, Gus Plath, Tony Fortez, Steve Senaney, Chuck Lightfoote, Michael White, Sean Quinn, Dave Peacock, Tom Doyle, Fred Ihrke, Mark Wesely and John Secrest.

THIS PICTURE CANNOT BE EXPLAINED, SO WE WILL JUST PASS IT OFF AS "SOME OF THE GUYS."

E. G. NEISON (The Shark) INSTRUCTS THE TROUBLE SHOOTERS ON THE FINE ART OF TIRE REPAIR!!

Next, we have to dedicate a few lines to our line members scheduled to leave us or that have already left us in the past month. Wayne Kemp and James Smith have already left the line and are returning to the states. Before the end of the next line period, we will say our good-byes to Jon Gripne, Bill Brown, Steve Talbott and Skip Roberts. They are also returning to the states for discharge. We doubt that anyone on the line would mind trading places with them. All we have is our future schedule: We plan to visit Hong Kong shortly and nobody should mind that due to the fact that the only place we've been to this cruise is the Philippines.

6

91

From the Ready Room

As we sit here in Cubi, happily sunning ourselves under the balmy tropical sun which has shone brilliantly since we arrived for the least ten seconds every day, we are all somewhat confused by rumors and doubt over what the future holds for us. Will Young Ben get married while he's in Hawaii? Will the Rat ever make it to Hong Kong? Will we ever find Dolan and Conway? Can the Oriskany's Navigator manage to get us to Hong Kong, or are we in fact doomed, as many now suspect to ride back and forth on tracks between Cubi and Yankee Station forever? Will there be a magic carpet and if so who will go? And of course, the question that's on everyone's lips, will Ted Kennedy ever be able to enjoy another cookout?

Word has it that our daily sorties are going to be cut during this next line period as part of the economy move. If so, it seems only reasonable that we have a small detachment here on the ship, consisting of 6 or 7 pilots and 5 birds and take the rest of the squadron back to Miramar. Then we could rotate replacements out here every month or two. But no, that wouldn't work either; then we wouldn't have enough J.O.'s on board for our most vital function, standing shore patrol and picket boat watches in Hong Kong.

Will success spoil Rick Parker? For the last week or two our stalwart operations officer (known affectionately as "Bud" to his close friends in the squadron) has taken over the lofty post of Acting CAG Ops, a position renowned as one of great power and responsibility and a stepping stone to greatness. Since taking this heavy burden on his shoulders, we have noticed a distinct gleam in his eye, a spring in his step and a new note of authority in his voice. We, of course, sincerely hope that he will remember the Red Flashes as he goes on to greater things (maybe even Air Force Staff College) and honor us from time to time with guest appearances at our frolicsome AOM's, perhaps even deigning to lay a few sea stories on us from that great wealth of Cobra-Lore.

Vocalist-of-the-month Honors for the month go to John Strahm, for a stirring rendition of "You'll Never Walk Alone". Great, John, just great, but could you sing a little louder next time?

A letter is now being circulated among the Red Flashes petitioning President Nixon to make some small economy move on the next moon shot such as saving some paint by painting "USA" a little smaller and using the money for a very good cause - to buy Ready Five a new movie projector. See the squadron rep now and add your name to the throng of irate movie fans.

7

NOW FOR ANOTHER EXCITING ADVENTURE FROM "THE MAINTENANCE CONTROL RED FLASHES"

As the days grew longer and the nights lonelier the men from Maintenance Control kept up with the pace of the war. Big Dick (ADCS GERRITSEN), our second in command was planning the move against the enemy while our leader Hank (LT. COIE), was looking into the rumors of snakes crawling up the landing gear of our fighting F4J's. The job was given to Davey Baby (AEC DAVIS), who has always had an eye for assignments of this importance. He was prepared with the latest in flight deck gear.

The night was one of the most horrifying of all nights, with no moon and very cold winds. While going up to the flight deck he encountered many dangers, such as passing through Animal Country, where they would kidnap by-passers and give them that terrifying bumpy leg. There was also the danger of passing through Brand "X" Country and lowering himself to such an act. But nothing could stop Davey Baby from continuing his ever so dangerous mission.

This was it, he had made it through Animal Country and was finally on the flight deck. His time of triumphant had come. He was going to walk across the flight deck and capture one of those deadful snakes. His heart was beating faster and faster. Time was drawing nearer when it happened. Davey Baby failed and was caught by one of the snakes across his ankle. Where had he failed. This was another victory for that deadly "Tie Down Snake".

While Davey Baby was going through his adventures, the other heros were busy fighting the war. Norb (ADCS HEILAND), our co-commander, along with Big Dick, was busy down in headquarters watching a secret film just flown in from Washington D. C.. How can we lose the war with three brilliant minds working together. There will never be men like Hank, Big Dick and Norb. When not on the flight deck they are with their men. What leaders, and to think they are on our side.

There are now in the ranks, three new promising heros. Frito Bendido Andy (AZ2 RONQUILLO) who fools the enemy pretending he is asleep and wakes up fighting like no other in History. After all his grandfather was Pancho Villa and his father is the owner of Taco Bell in California.

Our second new hero is Mony Mony Ken (AZ2 PARRISH) who will someday be as great as our own Hank. Playing the part as the everyday dumb American Mony Mony Ken has captured many with his outstanding skills. His hideout is the swanky Acey-Duecy Club. His code name is "Green Green Grass of Home". He has over come many crisis and won many victories for our side.

Last of the new heros is Chester (AZ3 DILLION), who has mastered the act of walking like a cripple and thus obtains head of the line everywhere he goes. For such acts he has been awarded the "Red Flash", a symbol of courage, strength and truth among men. HUD'N, HUD'N to our "Maintenance Control Heros"

By Frito Bendido Andy

8

PARALOFT PATTER

In starting, we in the "Loft" would like to welcome J. D. IAIN PR3 who reported to us from VA-122. We know that you will be a great asset to the shop. We are also looking to PR2 R. J. FLYNN's arrival. He is reporting in from PR "B" School. We understand he will soon be putting on another stripe. Previously, R. J. was with VF-126 at Fighter Town. Mike MOORE is looking forward to an early out in January to his education. Mike did an outstanding job of running the shop while PR1 GRISWOLD was in Danang for a week. Well done, Mike. We riggers are still trying to figure out if the VC are paying AME2 PRICE for all the fine work he is doing for us on the Beach Det. PR1 Paul MAGEL has left the shop and is now on his way to NAS PAX. Lots of Luck, Paul. We in the shop would like to help you the readers understand our job by explaining some our duties. We are responsible for the pilots' flight gear. It consists of the helmet, the oxygen mask, the oxygen breathing regulator, and the torso suit which is also the parachute harness. It has pockets on it in which the pilot can carry pencils, flares, also emergency radios you communicate with the ship or ground personnel in case of bail out. It also has an LPA-1 attached. The LPA-1 is a flotation device to be used in case the pilot ends up having to ditch in the water. There is also the "G" Suit which is used in case of extreme positive or negative "G's". It keeps blood from pooling in the pilot's stomach and prevents "black out". In the aircraft, we have the parachute to maintain. It is pulled out every 120 days, hung in a special drying tower and repacked. We also have the seat pan which the pilot sits on. In it is a one man life raft and different at-sea survival gear. We also take care of any sewing the pilot has which has to be done. Our shop motto is "You can depend on us to let you down". Until next month, so long from PR1 'Mr. Clean' GRISWOLD, Mike "Admiral" MOORE, FRAN and PR3 "J. D." IAIN.

RED FLASHES

EMERGENCY LEAVE - PNC F. M. "Cris" CRISTOBAL left on the 16th of this month on emergency leave. FITRON 194 wishes "Cris" godspeed.

NEW RED FLASH - SN William G. KEUNTJE was the father of a bouncing baby boy this month. Both wife and child are doing well.

9

"The talented, dedicated and hardworking members of CAG staff work day and night to make us the best air wing in the fleet".

"Vitalis actually holds hair in place while standing in front of this slightly under-powered F8J turning up at 100%."

10

THE HARD CORE RETURNS

By The Hard Core

The long forgotten crew (VF-194 Danang Bingo Det Alpha) returns to the Mighty "O". As the Mighty "O" pulled into Subic Bay to tie up, three hard-looking combat vets from the jungles were standing on the pier awaiting the Red Flashes' return to their second home. Dressed in combat fatigues, the three troupers, PR1 (Mr. Clean) GRISWOLD (O in C), AMH3 (Red Mountain) HAT-FIELD (XO), and AE3 LANDSIEDEL (MAINT OFF), had just returned from seven days at Danang, Vietnam.. In the seven days, the Hard Core accomplished the hard task of returning Red Flash "200" and its combat vet pilot LCDR Nigel (MAJ) MILLER to the ship. The aircraft was returned to the ship in out-standing working condition. The only thing that showed us on the air field was 'why'. The Mach I Fly Over with the gear down, CDR?

After two days of looking under rocks and in empty G.I. cans , we disco covered that two of our fellow red flashes, 'Rags' GAITHER and 'Butch' NOLL could no longer hack dodging rockets and bullets and somehow got a ride back out to the ship. After five days in our command bunker and numerous beer runs and one forty pounder later, we came to the bright conclusion that we had been forgotten. With this sad thought in mind, the crew was seen sway-ing down the streets at four in the morning driving the local MP's out of their minds.

After fixing an F-8 for VF-162 off the Ticc and packing a chute for VC-5, the VC-5 O in C big-dealed us a hop to Cubi in a VRC50 C-130. In ending this sad story we all agreed that if we had it to do over again, we wouldn't!

P.S. We can't really say that is not true Mr. Clean was seen kicking two vietnamese maidens down the road at one in the morning.

The RED LIGHTNING ILLUSTRATED is published monthly by the Legendary Red Lightnings of Fighter Squadron ONE HUNDRED NINETY FOUR and is a product of the Public Affairs Office in conjunction with the Admin Office.

ADVISOR: LT   Rocky ROCKWELL
EDITOR: YN2 David K. BOWMAN
STAFF ARTIST: DMSN James M. PETERS
TYPIST: SN Cris CRISTOBAL

CONTRIBUTORS

PR1 Joseph L. GRISWOOD   THE HARD CORE
ADJ2 Dale R. SETFORD   AZ2 Andy RONQUILLO
ADJ2 Lee W. GILBERTSON

Volume I Number 3 AUGUST 1969   A RED LIGHTNING PUBLICATION

11

September 1969

Once more the hottest-selling newstand item west of Olongapo and east of Cape Muy Ron is being loosed on the news-hungry public for its edification and amusement, the Pulitzer Prize reject, Red Lightning Illustrated, with a circulation numbered in the dozens. If the tone of this month's issue seems a bit more light-hearted than usual, it can probably be attributed to the fact that we have just finished our fourth line period and have just one more to go before the trip home.

The most exciting news of this line period, of course, was Lt. Mike Riddell's hasty exit of Red Flash 214 the other night followed by the good ol' nylon descent. Once more our confidence in Martin Baker has been enhanced by the flawless operation of his ejection seat. Also, a well done to the parachute riggers who packed his chute, Joe Griswold and Mike Moore.

Once again we have gone through a line period with truly outSTANDING maintenance. Our number of sorties lost due to maintenance was almost as low as the third line period, and the number of times we've had to launch the spare has fallen off to a trickle. Now if we can just manage to overcome the salt-water spray we've been getting up in the northern waters and the two-week lay-off in Sasebo, we should be able to make the next line period a new high in commitments made, plus. Maybe we'll even be able to pick up some more Feedbag sorties.

I'm afraid we owe everybody an apology for the delay in getting out our last issue, it was about two weeks late. It was partly a fault of the paper's management and partly due to a shortage of materials in the Oriskany print shop. We'll try not to let it happen again.

*   *   *   *   *   *   *   *

Hong Kong was, of course, great. I'm sure almost everybody in the squadron would like to go back someday. And I'm also sure that the merchants in the town will be glad to see us come back; any estimates of the amount of money we spent there would probably be too small. The important thing is, we had a good time and finally got to some port other than Cubi. Now we're about to pull into Sasebo, and according to the people who have been here before we can expect another great liberty. Everybody in the squadron's certainly earned it after that last line period. Also, we're planning a squadron party sometime while we're here, the date as yet unknown., but hopefully around the 26th. Chief Bonner will be over the side at first liberty call to make the arrangements. Anybody who takes pictures at the party and wants to get them in the next issue of the Red Lightning Illustrated, or any other pictures for that matter, either in Sasebo or out at sea, show them to Lt. Rockwell, TM2 Bowman, or PN2 Garrett. Black and white only.

-1-

By way of commercial, let me reiterate that this newsletter belongs to you, the members of the squadron, and it will only be as good as you make it. Any ideas, articles, cartoons, jokes, pictures or contributions of any kind are more than welcome from anybody. If you have anything to contribute at all, even if it's just a POD-type announcement, please see one of the people mentioned in the previous paragraph. At present, we are planning only one more issue this cruise, at the end of our last line period; but it's never too early to start thinking about next cruise and we might even come out with some during the turn-around if there's enough interest. By the way, the deadline for articles for that next issue will be 29 October.

I never know what to do with these spare parts.

-2-

Typical pre-launch
scene (left) showing
the arrangement of
the flight deck.

The cheerful, eager,
competent faces of the
maintenance personnel
greet the pilot as he
walks out to man his
aircraft. (below)

COMBAT
LAUNCH

Prior to start-up, a little
unwanted "F.O.D." (Flying
Object Damage) is removed
from the intake of the jet.
(left)

-3-

Pre-takeoff checks
completed, the pilot
awaits the signal from
the plane director to
taxi forward to the
catapult (above)

The photo bird,
who we'll be
escorting over
the beach, follows
close behind.
(right)

Finally the
chocks are
pulled and he
threads his way
up the flight
deck between
the other air-
craft. (above)

From zero to 150 mph
in about to seconds -
a ride like that would
cost at least 50¢ at
Coney Island. (left)

-|-

Homeward

KANSAS
PARSONS

Bound

AMC5 Howard Rice

17 November 1969 will be a big day for AMC5 Howard Rice. He'll be retiring from the U. S. Navy.

Chief Rice joined the Navy on 5 May 1943, going to Naval Air Station Corpus Christi not long afterward. During his long naval career, he served under Commander Fleet Air Japan; Commanding Officer, Naval Missile Center, Pt. Mugu, California; Fighter Squadron ONE HUNDRED TWENTY ONE; Helicopter Anti-Submarine Squadron TEN; Fighter Squadron TWO HUNDRED THIRTEEN and many other distinguished commands.

He has recieved the Navy Commendation Medal, the United Nations Medal, Korean Service Medal, Vietnam Service Medal, Vietnam Campaign Medal, Good Conduct Medal, and the National Defense Medal.

More recently, Chief Rice came to Fighter Squadron ONE HUNDRED NINETY FOUR in August of 1968. He reported for duty and was assigned the billet of Leading Chief. During his year in the squadron, he was with the squadron on many of its short deployments to nearby bases for gunnery and bomb exercises. When Fitron ONE NINE FOUR boarded USS ORISKANY in April, Chief Rice was there to coordinate the on-loading of equipment and the setting up of the personnel office.

At work in the Personnel Office

All during this cruise, Chief Rice served aboard the squadron organizing and coordinating working parties, inspections and the various other activities of the squadron and ship, and insured that a proper Plan of the Day was issued and all hands kept informed. On 15 October, Chief Rice will be flown off the ship for separation processing and the squadron will say good-bye to one of the best leading chiefs that it ever had. Good luck, Chief! HUD'N HUD'N!

-5-

Anchors Aweigh!

ADCS Norbert J. HEILAND, above, our Night Check Maintenance Chief, was sworn in by the skipper between launches on 7 September. The pace set by air operations and maintenance caused this ceremony to be a bit less formal than usual, and minutes later, the skipper was back in the cockpit and Chief HEILAND was back to the difficult task of keeping the birds up to HED'N BUD'N par.

PR1 Joseph L. GRISWOLD, left, our number one Rigger, shipped for 6 years on 15 July. Congratulations Mr. Clean.

QA Cage

By
Basel B. Mayer

This is a story about the eight people in Fighter Squadron ONE HUNDRED NINETY FOUR who have job of questioned popularity namely, Quality Assurance.

Someone has to be responsible for making sure that the maintenance performed on our aircraft is of high quality; this is our job. Actually, Quality Assurance is every man's responsibility. Quality in workmanship and material condition cannot be obtained solely through the Quality Assurance Division alone. It is the job of each man in the maintenance department.

There are seven guys assigned from the different shops to Quality Assurance. Our division officer is LT Michael W. O'BAR whose leadership has enabled our division to function to its fullest extent.

Chief DAVIS (better known as Davy) is our division chief. You will have to look hard to find a better guy! He is usually on the flight deck making sure everything is A-OK for launching the Red Flashes.

We have two first class petty officers, AMN1 JEFFERS (Alias Jeff) and AO1 HOLT. Jeff is in charge of inspecting flight controls, structures and corrosion control. This is a full time job which requires a good man to complete. Jeff has demonstrated more than once his ability to do this.

AO1 HOLT is replacing AO1 HOLTZER who was recently transferred. HOLT workes flight quarter hours, and has the important assignment of checking for safety while installing ordnance and making sure that safety always comes first

Finally, our three second class petty officers, and the Tech. Librarian.

AE2 PIERCE known as "Mike" , is in charge of Quality Assurance for the electricians. After hours provide just about enough time for Mike to read his motorcycle magazines and take pictures with his new "Canon". Mike is a short timer, just ask him, he will convince you of it! (This seems to be another of Mike's past-timer)

AME2 PRICE (D.G.) has just joined our division. He was flown aboard by a CCD from NAS Cubi Pt. D.G. inspects the canopy, ejection seats, cabin pressurization and insures maximum safety.

AT2 MAHALIK (known as Gramps at the beach Det and here on the ship) is in charge of quality assurance associated with the AT shop. He is taking the place of ATR2 KEELER, who is now separated from the NAVY.

-7-

By the way, we do have a little class in our division! AQF3 (BB) is the Squadron Tech Librarian. He recieves all incoming technical publications and directives and determines their application to Quality Assurance, recommending changes to these documents to the division chief (Davy). MEYER (BB) is also the division training petty officer.

The Quality Assurance division can only continue to provide "quality" factual information on workmanship and material condition only if you, the men who work with maintenance, demonstrate the determination that has thus far given Fighter Squadron ONE HUNDRED NINETY FOUR its present reputation of being "the best". HUD'N! HUD'N!

                    *   *   *   *

                    THE S.T.A.R. PROGRAM

                              By
                         FRC Robert Thomas

Thinking about getting out of the Navy? Or, do you have so long to go that you're not sure yet? Have something going for you on the outside? You have several things going for you if you make a career of the Navy. Don't think so? Try this on for size.

            SELECTIVE TRAINING AND RETENTION
     (S.T.A.R. PROGRAM) BUPERSINST 1133.13C (series)

The STAR Program is aimed primarily at retaining the electronics oriented ratings where the cost of training, in time and money, is high. It is applicable to any rating, however, for those who can qualify, and encourages personnel to identify as career designated early in their first enlistment. Reenlistment under this instruction qualifies personnel for career designation.

Some of the benefits are:

                    Persons in pay grade E-3

(a) Entitled to reenlistment courses, variable if eligible
(b) Guaranteed Class "A" School
(c) Automatic advancement to pay grade E-4 if eligible
(d) Personnel in pay grade E-3 who are automatically advanced
to E-4 are not eligible for addition benefits applicable to
personnel who reenlist in pay grades E-4 and E-5.

                    Persons in pay grade E-4

(a) Entitled to reenlistment courses, variable if eligible
(b) Guaranteed Class "B" or "C" School
(c) Automatic advancement to E-5 upon successful completion
of Class "B" School
(d) Proficieny pay if eligible

                                        -8-

S.T.A.R. (Cont.)

Persons in pay grade E-5

    (a) Entitled to reenlistment courses, variable if eligible
    (b) Guaranteed Class "B" School or "C" School
    (c) Proficiency pay if eligible

ELIGIBILITY FOR S.T.A.R. PROGRAM

All personnel of the Regular Navy, or Naval Reserve on active duty who desire to avail themselves of the various career incentives outlined herein may be recommended by their commanding officer to the Chief of Naval Personnel for career designation.

Qualifications for personnel who desire career designation under this instruction are as follows:

    (a) Personnel must have at least one year of active Naval service but no more than three years of active military service.
    (b) Personnel in pay grade E-5 must have no more than 42 months of active military service.
    (c) Requirements for Nuclear Power/Polaris vary.
    (d) Agree to enlist or reenlist in the Regular Navy for six years
    (e) Obtain BuPers permission prior to reenlisting
    (f) If unable to meet test score requirements for "A" School it is possible to recieve a waiver of up to ten points, or a retake of the basic battery test, where deserving.
    (g) Must meet minimum military behavior requirements for recommendation, and can be dropped for misconduct. The reenlistment contract remains valid if dropped from the program for misconduct unless being discharged for misconduct.
    (h) Personnel requesting school, which is guaranteed under the provisions of this instruction, must meet the obligated service requirements for entrance into such school as required by the Enlisted Transfer Manual.

If you've read this far, you at least have time to give thought to the subject. Have you honestly given this subject the consideration it deserves? If you'd like to know more, see the career counselor for the straight information.

-9-

106

PART TWO OF THE EXCITING ADVENTURES OF THE "MAINTENANCE CONTROL SUPER HEROES"

This was one our toughest assignments ever. Not only were our men fighting their own battles but were also doing the fighting for BRAND X. This was no easy task for us, but we had the ability and the spirit to do the job. Our leaders were doing a great job in keeping our Fighting F-8's in a great status and have in the past weeks kept them in a HUD'N HUD'N condition. HANK (LT COLE) was up day and night seeing that our schedule would be made. Big Dick (ADCS GERRITSEN) and Norb (ADCS HEILAND) were busy in keeping our underground posted on current crises. Up at headquarters, Chester (AZ3 DILLON) was intercepting the messages from the enemy and giving them to our underground. You can take it from me that this man has been doing a job expected from a Red Flash. Mony Mony Ken (AZ2 PARRISH) was also very busy on the homefield. Not only was he getting valuable information for us but he was also getting a new code book about intercommunication.

New to our group is a certain PR1 who keeps telling people he is first class P.O. and gives orders to our beloved Joe. Roger Ram Jet (PR1 FLYNN) will soon find out that it takes time and ambition to achieve that great goal and become a Red Flash. Joe (PR1 GRISWOLD) will show him in his own mysterious way. We know you'll do a good job on him, Joe, like always.

While some of us were busy with our work we were forgetting to finish and complete our work. But our team is prepared for this with the great mind of Davey Baby, better known as Stress Fastener Davis (AEC DAVIS). He would go out and find our mistakes and would with his mild temper ask the different persons to fix them. Yes, old Davey Baby would get up in the middle of the night and eagerly help our top officials.

Frito Bandito Andy (AZ2 RONQUILLO) has been up to his old tricks and has been getting away with supplies from the enemy and making deals with Chilli "T". Chilli "T" is always out for the fast buck. Chilli "T" (AK3 TORRES) is a very important person to us. Here they are folks, two of a kind. Frito Bandito Andy and Chilli "T". VIVA ANDY and CHILLI "T"!

We are now looking forward in the beautiful country of Japan. In about two more months, the hearths of our country will be ours and we would have known that we did our part of the job in keeping our promise to the people of the free world. People may say we are no better than any other squadron but to us we are the best due to the fact that we have people like Hank, Big Dick and Norb and Davey. It is up to these men to keep our faith in this squadron and we are showing them that we do have the faith by being the best. I feel proud to say we have the best in the U. S. Navy. Everybody has done their part from the newest Airman to the Commanding Officer. I can only say it is because we try harder.

Good Show Amigos
Andy Ronquillo Jr.

PARALOFT PATTER

ROGER RAMJET & ADMIRAL MOORE

"Welcome aboard", said Mr.
Clean. The only thing going
through my mind was "Charlie
Two didn't land anything like
a P2V-7." Ah, but the memories
of two turning and two burning.

As I looked around, it came to me
that Admiral MOORE's briefing was
true; this "O" Boat was actually
moving. I already knew these flat
things moved. I just wasn't a
part of it until now. I felt bad
about not thanking the Admiral for
his fine briefing; not that I
didn't try. A thorough search of
NAS Cubi was hopeless, for he was
nowhere to be found. I can't
imagine where he could have been.
When talking with him, I thought
it kind of strange the way he
answered questions about Red Flashes—
I mean what kind of an answer is
Hud'n Hud'n?

"You can depend on us to let you down"

Mr. Clean seemed glad to see me
arrive, muttering something about no more 18 hour days...he could get a
little sleep now. I agree he could use some beauty sleep, but sleeping
every day for the remainder of the cruise probably won't help much.

To all you Red Flash Salts, I would like to thank you for showing this
green-horn around. It's a nice place you have here, but myself, I
wouldn't want to stay long. I might recommend you ask the Navy to put
a little room between the deck and the overhead. It would be a little easier
on my head and Mr. Clean wouldn't be standing in the passageway all the
time laughing.

Ah, but the memories of two turning and two burning.

Mr. Clean is trying to get my name known among the Red Flashes. He's trying
extra-hard around the ready room—and my name's not Roger Ramjet!

I'm sure looking forward to Sasebo and the squadron party. It will be good
to leave the Mighty "O" for a spell on solid ground. Let's see if I have
this straight—now, you salute the ensign and then the OOD or is that when
you come back? Ah, but the memories of two turning and two burning. Arduous
sea duty, you know!

-11-

PR3 (LOIS) LAIN

As most of you know, being sent TAD to a different work center or organization offers both an opportunity to become familiar with the different areas of your work and be able to assess for yourself the importance of these different organizations and the part you play in them. Currently, I am TAD to IM-2 Division in the Paraloft and the part I play is varied depending upon the amount of work. Our organization level is intermediate, which means that anything beyond the squadron capabilities is sent to us. We pack and perform modifications on parachutes, test and maintain flotation gear and present our sewing skills to any who need them. Contrary to popular belief, ship's company personnel are highly capable and (this is the part I like) are very dependent on all the air wing to earn their day's wages. So help them out.

THE HARD CORE

Well, now that the last line period is almost upon us, we really feel we are getting short. However, lets all remember safety when working around the the ship. We are looking forward to another high grade on the aircraft inspection in Sasebo. See all of you good people in Sasebo! Good night shoe shine girl!

PR1 GRISWOLD (Mr. Clean)
PR1 FLYEN (Roger Ramjet)
PR3 (LOIS) LAIN
PRAN (ADMIRAL) MOORE

* * * * * *

HUD'N HUD'N ORDNANCE SHOP

AO3 D. S. KIMBALL

No, the Ordnance Shop is not dead; we are alive and kicking. Due to our shortage of men and our work load, we have fallen behind on the squadron newsletter. But we will try to keep up in the future.

New Petty Officers in the shop are WILSON AO3 (finally), HARPER AO3, and WHITLEY AO3. All were anxious to sew on their crows and to their complete surprise, the line shack held a formal reception for these lucky few.

Word has reached us on Joe PEPP. Joe is the father of an 8 pound 6 ounce baby girl. Congratulations Joe! Joe is also getting an early release from active duty, so we of VF-191 Ordnance wish Joe all the luck in the world as he leaves the Navy and enters civilian life. (The same from the entire squadron HUD'N HUD'N!)

We are all looking forward to Japan and if anyone has any extra Special Request chits, they could drop them by the shop! So nothing else new from the ORD Shop except that we are still sparing for the "Feedbags" (VF-191).

-12-

The logistics helos of HC-7 make daily trips between the many ships in the Tonkin Gulf carrying mail, passengers and much needed airplane parts.

Re-fueling at sea from the USS ASHTABULA.

-13-

SEAT SHOP SKINNY   AME-3 MIKE LeSAGE

By the time this issue hits the newstands, we should be starting our
fifth and final line period. Of course, we all look forward to our
return home in a month and a half. The AME shop has been a busy one this
fourth period. Our fearless leader AME2 Jerry (Stanley) Salter has
left us. He is in Memphis going to AME "B" School and from there he goes
to Pensacola, Florida where he'll stay until he gets out. By the way,
that's home, for him. So now we have a new shop supervisor, AME3 Rolland
(Elmer) POPE, yes its true. Since Stan left, the work has piled up on
Elmer, and his only two workers are AME3 Robie (Mattress Back) ROBERTSON
a new arrival to HUD'N HUD'N, and Mike (Bootcamp) LESAGE, who we just got
from the Lox Crew. Don (D.G.) PRICE, some of you know him as "Torch", just
checked back from the Beach Det.

About the worst part about our job is the shop, because we've got to
share it with VA-192 (Yellow Worms) and VF-191 (Brand X).

If a guy can manage to get through the day listening to the heavy
sounds of Elmer POPE, or the Jazz sounds from Mike LESAGE, or the country
western from Robbie ROBERTSON, or the folk from Don PRICE, he's doing
good. All in all the shop is okay, but a couple more AME's would do the
trick.

Several Red Flashes in
the Power Plants Shop
were photographed here
recently in the middle
of a vigorous surge of
effort.

-14-

111

MOTOR MENDERS

This is your foreign war correspondent Fat Albert, back from the jungles of Vietnam. Yes, folks, while the ship was busy in P.I. and Hong Kong, the highly skilled talent of Fat Albert, Roy Gaither and of course a 13 year highly trained Navy Metalsmith James (Flash) Jordan were in Danang, Vietnam fixing A/C 201 in between rocket attacks and beer breaks during which time Fat Albert was awarded the title of lightning because of his speed runs to the bunker during the fireworks display.

When the ship arrived back on the line, the call went out to retrieve those great dashing war veterans to help with the destruction that had hit out great air force of plighty underpowered F8-J's. As we came in staggering numbers back to the ship, we discovered our second forcers Cliff HEAD, Earl BOHANON, Leo NULL, Chuck DALECKI, D.D. DUAX, and our newest acquisition W. B. DAY, sleeves rolled up, elbow-deep in grease.

After a careful estimate of the damage, it looked like one FOD, two CSD changes, two fuel control changes, two section change. (For the folks at home, this amounts to five engine pulls--which in plane talk is work.) All in all, people are slowly discovering that the planes are not put in the air with a few magic words but a lot of back breaking temper raising work. But we can hack it!

-15-

REFLECTIONS IN A LIGHTNING BOLT

BY: Lt. Norm Franklin

As this cruise draws into the last line period and our return to the States is in a matter of weeks, I think it would be good to reflect on some of the things we have learned again about our squadron as a whole and as individuals.

We have seen Fighter Squadron ONE HUNDRED NINETY FOUR put forth an excellent effort as documented by our main product as a fighter outfit, that is combat sorties with parts in short supply and exceedingly short turn around times for maintenance, our team effort has more than met our commitments and in many cases we've carried the load for other fighter outfits. As a squadron, then, we've seen what pride and professionalism in a team spirit can produce. I hope we've learned this for our future challenges, so that we'll meet them and complete them with vigor.

Equally as important is what we've learned as individuals about ourselves. We sign our names in more ways than just by pen and ink. Every time a piece of work gets done, or an aircraft takes off that we've worked on or got the parts for, your signature is a part of that job. Even a support function such as baking the food that goes into the mechs or cleaning the shirts in the laundry or swabbing the decks in our compartments—your work and effort and enthusiasm is your signature. And combined, this represents the quality of Fighter Squadron ONE HUNDRED NINETY FOUR as a squadron. I hope we've also learned then about what we can expect from ourselves; the really fine job we can do when under pressure and working under less than desirable conditions.

As a Junior Officer I've enjoyed tremendous association with our fighter squadron. I've had absolute confidence in the products of your labor, because you have had the confidence and pride to make it right, in yourselves. The men of ONE NINETY FOUR stand out because they are outstanding. That will be one of the thoughts I'm truly proud to take back from the cruise.

-16-

113

I have been one of the most avid fans of firing the guns out on the way back from Barcap station, weather recce, or any other of hop, just to see how they work. But after a talk with the guys down in our ordnance shop, I've found that they'd rather we keep this activity to a minimum until the last half of the next line period. Also , they prefer that we do it on one of the last two hops of the day so they dont have to worry about reloading it for the next launch.

The best movie of the line period turned out to be "Daddy's Gone ahunting" with the Air Force drug abuse film a close second. All the rest were tied for last, with the possible exception of "Magus", which had a couple of redeeming scenes.

Here's one for the guys in the O's "A" Division; with a 5½ month turn-around coming up, would it be too much to hope that perhaps some of these old pre World War I air conditioners be replaced by new ones before the next cruise? Specific cases in point are A-310, which serves stateroom 318 and two others, and the old workhorse in Ready Five, which has been leaking for months and finally burned out a compressor about a week ago. We really appreciate the fast repair job by the electricians but it seems clear that brand new units are needed all over the ship, like the ones in forward officers' country. Let's hope something is done about it by the supply guys as soon we get back to the states rather than waiting till April when it's too late.

A retraction is in order from the last issue; due to a misprint, the XO's children were listed as "Patricia, Michelle and Michael", when in fact the first name should have been Patrick. Sorry about that, Pat; hope you dont cancel you subscription.

The RED LIGHTNING ILLUSTRATED is published monthly by the Legendary Red Lightnings of Fighter Squadron ONE HUNDRED NINETY FOUR and is a product of the Public Affairs Office in conjunction with the Admin Office.

ADVISOR:	LT Rocky ROCKWELL
EDITOR:	YN2 David K. BOWMAN
STAFF ARTIST:	DMSN James M. PETERS
TYPIST:	SN Cris CRISTOBAL

CONTRIBUTORS

LT Norm FRANKLIN	ADJ2 Dale R. SETFORD
PHC Robert THOMAS	ADJ2 Lee W. GILBERTSON
FR1 Joe GRISWOLD	AMH3 Michael LESACK
HE1 R.J. FLINN	AQF3 Basel B. METER
PN2 Willie A. GARRETT	AO3 D. S. KIMBALL
AX2 Andy RONQUILLO	ADJ3 R. L. ALLEN

Volume I Number 4 SEPTEMBER 1969   A RED LIGHTNING PUBLICATION

-18-

I have been one of the most avid fans of firing the guns out on the way back from Barcap station, weather recce, or any other of hop, just to see how they work. But after a talk with the guys down in our ordnance shop, I've found that they'd rather we keep this activity to a minimum until the last half of the next line period. Also , they prefer that we do it on one of the last two hops of the day so they dont have to worry about reloading it for the next launch.

The best movie of the line period turned out to be "Daddy's Gone aHunting" with the Air Force drug abuse film a close second. All the rest were tied for last, with the possible exception of "Magus", which had a couple of redeeming scenes.

Here's one for the guys in the O's "A" Division; with a 5½ month turnaround coming up, would it be too much to hope that perhaps some of these old pre World War I air conditioners be replaced by new ones before the next cruise? Specific cases in point are A-310, which serves stateroom 318 and two others, and the old workhorse in Ready Five, which has been leaking for months and finally burned out a compressor about a week ago. We really appreciate the fast repair job by the electricians but it seems clear that brand new units are needed all over the ship, like the ones in forward officers' country. Let's hope something is done about it by the supply guys as soon we get back to the states rather than waiting till April when it's too late.

A retraction is in order from the last issue; due to a misprint, the XO's children were listed as "Patricia, Michelle and Michael", when in fact the first name should have been Patrick. Sorry about that, Pat; hope you dont cancel you subscription.

The RED LIGHTNING ILLUSTRATED is published monthly by the Legendary Red Lightnings of Fighter Squadron ONE HUNDRED NINETY FOUR and is a product of the Public Affairs Office in conjunction with the Admin Office.

ADVISOR:	LT Rocky ROCKWELL
EDITOR:	YN2 David K. BOWMAN
STAFF ARTIST:	DMSN James M. PETERS
TYPIST:	SN Cris CRISTOBAL

CONTRIBUTORS

LT Norm FRANKLIN	ADJ2 Dale R. SETFORD
PHC Robert THOMAS	ADJ2 Lee W. GILBERTSON
PR1 Joe GRISWOLD	AMH3 Michael LESAGE
PR1 R.J. FLINN	AQF3 Basel B. MEYER
PH2 Willie A. GARRETT	AO3 D. S. KIMBALL
AZ2 Andy RONQUILLO	ADJ3 R. L. ALLEN

Volume I Number 4   SEPTEMBER 1969   A RED LIGHTNING PUBLICATION

-18-

From the Ready Room

An era has ended in VF-194 with the departure of "The Rat", LCDR Tom Reed, the last remaining Red Flash pilot from the 1967 cruise when they used to bomb Hanoi and Haiphong. The cheese-eater departed ORISKANY on a COD bound for Cubi sometime in the middle of the line period. In his new position of authority at COMFAIRMIRAMAR, whatever it will be, we feel confident that he'll take care of his old Red Flash buddies ith good deals like per-diem in El Centro, etc., right Rat? Nigal Miller will also be leaving soon, before we leave Sasebo as a matter of fact. I'm sure the poor ol' Maj will be broken-hearted at having to leave his pals on the "Oh" or "O" or however you spell it. There have been reports, as yet unconfirmed, that he was seen late one night running up and down the passageways, flapping his arms and yelling "Zoom!" and "Roger wilco, over and out!" in preparation for his upcoming duty station at Otis Air Force Base. One of the LSO phone talkers even reported that he turned his landing light on for his last two trips and took a two-mile groove.

The saddest event of this line period, without a doubt was the loss of a true friend who served us well and for the whole cruise was a warm and cheery reminder of the good things in life. I'm referring, of course, to the indoor-outdoor carpet that we laid in the ready room on the way to Hawaii. The design was called "Indian Corn", and although it had its detractors (some irreverent souls seemed to think it looked like the whole squadron had gotten sick all at once and had never cleaned it up) there was hardly a dry eye in the house when we had to dispose of it a couple of weeks ago. No one's really sure just why the black oil pumping room next door to ready five overflowed one night during a movie, but the result was the complete inundation of our rug, along with several ready room chairs, with Navy Special Fuel Oil. There was only one thing to do with it acter that, and this was taken care of with hardly a splash one dark night by some of the hard working J.O.'s. It was last seen being nibbled at hungrily by a school of adolescent Jew Fish (Side note: A hearty well done to Ed Cruz, SD3, the best ready room cleaner on the ship, who did a really outstanding job of laying red and black tile in the ready room after the rug was gone. This job required not only skill in laying tile, but also a great deal of tact, since he had to pretend to be following the directions of the bungling new first lieutenant, Young Ben Franklin, while actually ignoring him and doing it the right way.)

Animal Talk

By Dale Setford & Lee Gilbertson

Here we are again folks, with another edition of Animal Talk. Well, we have finally made it outside of the Philippines with a one week trip to Hong Kong. Everybody enjoyed themselves to the greatest extent, bought stuff they didn't need and drank a little which they did need. Our line division had a party in the "Cave Bar" in downtown Hong Kong and that turned out to be a fantastic time for all. Even our chief who was there with his bermuda shorts and hairy legs had a good time. Of course, everybody got back to the ship safely, so all was well.

Then, too, all good things must come to an end so we departed Hong Kong, heading again for Yankee Station. We had 35 days at sea staring us in the face and expected the worst. Within these 35 days we lost some more people to civilian life—Jon Gripne, Bill Brown, Skip Roberts, and Kenneth Keber.

Our line period started out as usual with our 2 crew system. After our first week, due to the loss of men to civilian life, we returned to a one crew system and that really put it on us. It was then back to the old flight quarters to flight quarters game. We started out a little slow that as usual we proved we could hack it. The trouble shooters five say they are so darn good and their is so perfect that they cant write an article without really bragging. Oh well! We will see what happens on our last line period.

Next is our line crew points of interest from our last line period. We recieved two new crew members; Jeff Mahalik and Lee (Slim) Gray. We were all very happy to welcome them to the Legendary Red Lightning Line Crew Initiation. Kangaroo Court was held and brought to order by the Honorable Judge Uncle Mike. Both defendants were found guilty by same and sentenced accordingly. Needless to say, the sentence was carried out with great vigor and enthusiasm. With all anxieties relieved, the daily routine was resumed.

August 16th was another great day for the line crew; the Honorable Judge Mike White, David Peacock and Fred Ihrke sewed on their third class crows.

Everyone is looking forward to going to Japan, which will be the first time we've been there this cruise. Many will see Japan for the first time and others their second and third time but all will enjoy it, needless to say.

Young John Seorest is looking for a vice-presidency in any available firm in the San Diego area, as he will be getting out of the Navy next month.

-19-

June 1970

WEST PAC '70

by
LCDR Jon C. KERNS

Once again the challenge, adventure and awe of the sea have drawn the officers and men of VF-194 to the West Pacific. In order to record all events and to report them worldwide, the Red Lightning Illustrated has again started its minds to working and its presses to humming. For the period of this issue we said farewell to San Francisco and the loved ones we left behind, transited the Pacific with a stop in Hawaii and finally a last minute respite in Cubi before assuming the duties of the line.

No one can say that we didn't come through with the good ole' Hud'n Hud'n spirit during our Operational Readiness Exercises (ORE) off Hawaii the 24th and 25th of May. VF-194's maintenance was outstanding resulting in many flight hours and a great showing for the Red Flashes.

Liberty for two days in Hawaii was well deserved. From the comments heard around the squadron, a good time was had by many.

From Hawaii, we set sail into the setting sun toward the West Pacific. The 10 day crossing was long and hard with the many alert conditions. However, there was time for holiday routine at times and many Red Lightnings took advantage of the warm temperatures and fair seas to sunbathe and lounge about the deck.

It cannot be said that VF-194 lacks strength in leadership as witnessed by our Executive Officer's "Man of Steel" program of flight deck running, weight lifting and various bend-overs. (See photo at right) It's a matter of fact that many Red Flashes were seen jogging, running and playing ball around the flight deck during our 10 day transit.

It was a great relief when mail call was finally heard some two days out of Cubi Point. The Philippines were a welcome sight as we docked. Our activities at Cubi were full of preparations for our upcoming line period. The pilots went to Jungle Survival School and received many lectures concerning conditions and procedures in Southeast Asia. Maintenance was busy preparing our birds for a demanding line period. On the 10th of June we left for two days of operations off the Philippines in order to be fully prepared for the Tonkin Gulf. Now we look forward to a successful line period and a good rest back at Cubi.

-1-

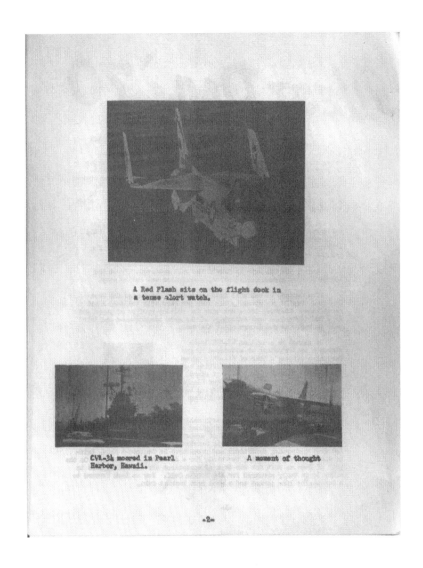

A Red Flash sits on the flight deck in a tense alert watch.

CVA-34 moored in Pearl Harbor, Hawaii.

A moment of thought

-2-

WELL DONE

A well done from Fighter Squadron ONE HUNDRED NINETY FOUR to the men who received awards on board USS ORISKANY (CVA-34) on 29 May 1970. All hands mustered on the flight deck where at 1545 Commander J. P. VINTI, the Commanding Officer presented the following awards to members of the command:

Naval Commendation Medal - AO2 Robert ANDERSON (See Page 5)
Naval Air Medal - AO2 Robert ANDERSON (See page 5)
Letter of Commendation for December 22 1969 Crash at NAS MIRAMAR -

AKAN Mark W. MCDONALD	ADJ3 Richard L. ALLEN
AK2 Mario S. TORRES	ADJ3 Earl BOHANNON
AQF3 Wallace E. BACON	ADJ2 James W. CRUMLY
ADJ1 Everett D. ADOLPH	ADJ3 Michael R. PEDERSEN
AQF3 James D. SPECHT	ADJ3 Douglas DUAX
ADJC Melvin DIAMOND	AZ2 Amado RONQUILLO
YN2 David K. BOWMAN	ADJ2 Ronald P. BABCOCK
AKC Cruz R. CUIZON	AK3 Lee R. GRAY
ASE2 David C. JEWELL	AMS3 L. R. THOMPSON
ATN3 David G. PEACOCK	AMS1 Hugh G. JENNINGS
AMS3 Thomas P. DOYLE	AMS2 Michael E. SANDERS
ATR2 Mark A. WESELY	AMS2 William F. HAIKY
AA Robert E. SHOLTY	AN Carl L. PERES
AMS3 David J. ROSS	AQ1 James S. SHIFLER
AOAN Raymond W. WIBE	AN Thomas L. MIKICAREK
AO1 Lloyd R. JOHNSON	

Good Conduct Medal

ADCS Norbert HEILAND	AO1 L. R. JOHNSON
ATN3 J. R. EVANS	ADJC Melvin DIAMOND

Advancement Certificates to Petty Officer First Class - AQ1 J.S. SHIFLER

Advancement Certificates to Petty Officer Second Class -

ADJ2 J. W. CRUMLY   AO2 R.T. ANDERSON
AK2 M.S. TORRES
ASE2 D.C. JEWELL
ATN2 S.P. SENSNEY

Advancement Certificates to Petty Officer Third Class -

ADJ3 Douglas DUAX
AMS3 L.R. THOMPSON
AMS3 D.J. ROSS

-3-

121

Plane Captain of the Month - ATN2 D.G. PEACOCK

Sailor of the Month - ASE2 David C. JEWELL

Pictured above are, front row, left to right: AKC C.R. CUIZON, ADJC M. DIAMOND, ADCS N.J. HEILAND; second row, left to right: AMS2 W.T. HALEY, YN2 D.K. BOWMAN, ATR2 M.A. WESELY, AMSJ T.P. DOYLE, AK2 M.S. TORRES, ADJ1 E.D. ADOLPH, AN C.L. PERES, AQF3 W.E. BACON, AQF3 J.D. SPECHT and ATN2 S.P. SENSNEY; third row, left to right: AQF2 J.N. STRAND, AA R.E. SHOLTY, AOAN R.W. WISE, ADJ3 Earl BOHANNON, ADJ3 D.D. DUAX, ATN3 D.G. PEACOCK, ASE2 D.C. JEWELL, AMS1 H.G. JENNINGS, AMS3 D.J. ROSS, AMS3 L.R. THOMPSON and AMSAN R. A. RAYMOND; back row, left to right: AQ1 J.S. SHIPLER, AMS2 L.W. JOHNSON, ATN2 J.R. EVANS, ADJ2 J.W. CRUMLY, ADJ3 R.L. ALLEN, ADJ3 M.R. PEDERSEN, AMS2 M.E. SANDERS, AKAN M.W. MCDONALD, AE3 L.R. GRAY, AO2 R.T. ANDERSON and AZ2 A. RONQUILLO.

-4-

122

AO2 T.L. HAND

Our hearty congratulations go out to a newly acquired member of our squadron, AO2 Robert "Andy" ANDERSON. At our last awards ceremony (See page 3) Petty Officer ANDERSON received triple honors. For his outstanding work while attached to Helicopter Attack (Light) Squadron THREE in Vietnam, he earned a field promotion to Aviation Ordnanceman Second Class. As if this wasn't enough, ANDERSON received his Second through Twenty-ninth Air Medals. Andy was ready to settle for this, but our Commanding Officer, CDR J. P. VINTI, had one more award. For his meritorious achievements while in combat, Andy received the Navy Commendation Medal with Combat "V" device.

Andy began his naval career on 22 August 1967. After completing his recruit training in San Diego, he attended Class "A" School in Jacksonville, Florida. Upon graduation, he received orders to PATRON THIRTY-ONE at Naval Air Station North Island in San Diego. It was at PATRON THIRTY-ONE that Petty Officer ANDERSON volunteered for duty in Vietnam.

AO2 ANDERSON and his recent bride, Carmine, have a home in Norco, California.

-5-

RED FLASH PILOTS WELCOME RADM RANGE TO USS GRIMANY — On 25 May 1970, the legendary Red Lightnings of Fighter Squadron ONE HUNDRED NINETY FOUR welcomed RADM RANGE aboard USS GRIMANY after he relieved RADM ISAMAN as COMMANDER CARRIER DIVISION SEVEN. Pictured above were, front row, left to right: LT W.C DEREK, LCDR L.J. JACKSON, CDR J.W. RYAN, the Executive Officer, CDR J.P. VINTI, the Commanding Officer, LCDR I.C. ERMIS and LT J.T. PHARNEY; top row, left to right: LT G.D. CROMELL, LTJG D.G. PRIEST, LT E.G. COIN, LTJG R.A. PARKER, LTJG R.K. BARTO, LT F.W. SAGE, LT J.R. ROCKWELL, LT D.A. MILLER, CWO2 T.W. TUDOR, LTJG D.J. CARPOWICH, LT R.V. JOHNSON, LTJG A.L. ERIKSON and LTJG J.C. JOHNSON.

By
TN2 D. K. BORMAN

Paradise HAWAIIAN STYLE

Shortly after the gangplank went down that sunny day in late
May, I went ashore. As I reached the pier, suitcase in one hand,
camera bag in the other, my sister-in-law ran to meet me, a big
smile on her face, and threw a lei of bright flowers over my head.
We had a lot to talk about; and as we drove through the colorful
streets of Honolulu, we reminisced over old times.

Soon, Honolulu fell behind and wavering fields of lush green
sugar cane surrounded us. Mile after mile passed and all I could
see was sugar cane, pineapple plants and the deep red Hawaiian
soil. In the distance, the mountains, shrouded in mist, stood
guard over the island.

To our left, the glittering azure sea gently chided the shore.
Sunbathers dotted the gleaming white beach. A cool breeze swept in
from the ocean. It wasn't long before we turned off the main road,
went down the narrow unpaved street, turned again and parked in
front of the small pleasant bungalo surrounded with colorful tropical
flowers. There was an air of peace and tranquility about the place;
birds chirped gaily in the trees, in the distance I could hear the
surf.

We spent the rest of the afternoon in the house sipping cold
drinks, eating fresh pineapple and talking. That evening, after my
brother had come home from his ship, we had dinner, sat in the
living room with the phonograph turned on low and talked into the
night.

In the next few days, I saw the paradise that was Hawaii; the
mountains, the beaches, the endless pineapple fields, Diamondhead.
We slept in the mornings; and in the afternoons we drove around the
island exploring and stopping at some of the beaches to splash in
the warm tropical water. When evening came, we would drive to the
quiet empty beach near the bungalo and swim until past sunset in the
incredibly warm ocean. At last, tired and hungry, we would drive
home.

Day's end would find us in the living room, listening to records,
reminiscing over the past, wondering about the future occasionally to
strain our ears and listen to the sounds of the warm tropical night.

-7-

125

KN©W Y©UR LINE
ANiMALS
By
Lt Rocky ROCKWELL

Back underneath the lumber three wire on the 02 level, there is a spacious little 30' by 20' oven known affectionately to its inhabitants as compartment C-0224-4L. Within this humble yet inviting little room can be found, in addition to a refrigerator, tie-down chains, cans of waterless cleaner and countless numbers of rags; an assortment of humans, sub-humans, and super-humans (depending on how long they've been working) that defies descript- ion. For this cozy little oven is the VF-194 Line Shack and it h houses the Legendary Line Animals (known better to the Personnel Office and EPDOPAC as the Line Division, with its Plane Captain and Troubleshooter branches, known to Chief ROHRER and his computers as Work Centers 310 and 320. Going by individual handles such as "Face", "Grid", "Fat Albert", "The Kid", "Uncle Mike", and "Frog", these 15 Plane Captains, 6 Troubleshooters and their supervisors make up one of the most vital and hard-working shops in the squadron. Not to take any credit away from the superb work done by the other fine divisions in our Red Lightning Maintenance Department, it is never-the-less the plane captains and troubleshooters who are the last ones the pilot sees before he goes off the catapult and the first he sees after he traps back aboard. Without the careful, conscientious pre-flight and post-flight inspections by the plane captains and the quick, efficient servicing and last minute repairs by the troubleshooters, sometimes fighting the clock to get a launch out, we would be unable to maintain the professional tempo of operations characteristic of the Red Lightnings.

The purpose of this column, which I hope will appear in each issue of the Red Lightning Illustrated, is to introduce a couple of these plane captains and troubleshooters and tell a little bit about them so that the pilots and the rest of the squadron will have a little better idea just who these guys are who clean their airplanes, swign off their "A" Sheets, service their air bottles and give them that final "thumbs up" on the cat.

ATN3 David G. PEACOCK

Dave PEACOCK, VF-194's Plane Captain of the Month for the month of April 1970 is a 24 year old southerner from the small town of Itta Bena, Mississippi. After graduating from La Flame County High School in 1964 and spending two years at Mississippi Delta Junior College in Moorehead, Mississippi, Dave joined the Navy and went to boot camp at the Great Lakes Training Center. After AT "A" School in Memphis and 8 weeks TAD with VF-124, he came to the Red Lightnings in March 1969. He became a qualified plane captain during our 1969

-8-

cruise and although he made third class petty officer in August 1969, he has remained a plane captain by choice and is certainly one of our finest. His aircraft is NM 202, which is flown by the XO, who requested him personally.

Dave is the second youngest in a family of nine (six boys and three girls) and grew up on his father's cotton and soybean farm in Itta Bena. He lists as his favorite activities hunting, fishing and archery, the first two of which he says, are much better in Mississippi than Southern California.

Dave has been married two years now and will be getting out of the Navy in March 1972. Upon separation, he hopes to attend Mississippi State University and study agriculture, with a mind to becoming a soil conservation specialist.

ASE2 Dave JEWELL

One of the biggest problems confronting a squadron's maintenance department while ashore, is the procurement and care of ground support equipment such as buffers, NC-5's and air compressors — usually known as "yellow gear". During our last turn around period at Miramar, the man almost exclusively in charge of our yellow gear was David JEWELL, ASE2. The fine job done by JEWELL with the yellow gear under somethings less than ideal conditions, plus his dilligent work with the line's 3-M documentation helped earn him the well-deserved title of VF-194 "Sailor of the Month" for the month of April 1970.

Unlike PEACOCK, JEWELL's interests run to the mechanical rather than agricultural. He has worked as a Ford Service Salesman in Kalamazoo, Michigan and his home town of Rochester New York and after getting out of the Navy in November of 1971, he hopes to go back into the auto business and eventually get his own dealership.

After graduating from Gates-Chili High School in Rochester, Dave attended Morrisville College in New York for two years, Western Michigan University for one year and then joined the Navy. After "A" School in Memphis, he spent a year with AMD Ground Support at NAS Key West, then came to VF-194 in October 1969. Since Dave is a ground support equipment specialist rather than a plane captain or troubleshooter, he will spend this cruise with our beach det at Cubi Point taking care of our yellow gear situation there will agree he has his work cut out for him.

-9-

127

Anchors Aweigh!

By
AZ2 Andy RONQUILLO

MAINTENANCE CONTROL, Q/A AND D/A GOOD GUYS

Hello, Amigos! Here we are again aboard the USS ORISKANY, the Mighty "O" as we call her. For a few of us, this will make the third time we have deployed with Fitron 194 to WestPac.

As you well know, we left Alameda, May 14th and headed to the beautiful land of the hula girls and palm trees, Hawaii, island of the sun. As we steamed away, many of us had received her golden touch of tropical sun.

We are now preparing for our assigned tasks and hope we can help bring a peaceful end to this war. Before we go to the combat zone, we had to stop in the Philippine Islands. There we off-loaded the check crew and picked up supplies. We were inport for three days. I will now introduce to you the good guys. The number one man is "Norb the Great" (ADCS HEILAND) who is our maintenance chief. The others in our group are as follows:

"Curly"	ADJC DIAMOND	"Chester"	AZ3 DILLON
"Snoopy"	AEC DAVIS	"Mustang Mush"	ATN3 McKISSICK
"Bonnie of Clyde"	AZC BONNER	"Tex"	AN EPPS
"N.I.S."	AKC CUIZON	"Murf the Surf"	ADJAN MURPHY
"Fred Farrel			
Farkel"	AEL FARRELL		
"Blue Jackets"	AMH1 CARR		
"Chilly T"	AK2 TORRES		

And yours truly "Frito Bandido" (AZ2 RONQUILLO). Before I go on "Snoopy" would like for everbody to know he received orders to NAS Norfolk, Virginia. We hope that in the coming months we will be able to bring a smile to your homes with our issue of the squadron newspaper. With this, I leave you until next time. Adios to all of you and good night "Big Dick" wherever you are.

-10-

128

Greetings *from the* RAT·PAC

AO3 Larry WAUTLET

Here we are again folks, aboard the USS ORISKANY. We've finally made it through all the inspections, carrier qualifications and have our new men catching on somewhat.

There is a big change of personnel from last year's fighting "ordies". Our dearly beloved Chief JOHNSON has finally left us. A lot of the old guys really miss him alot and just can't seem to get going without him.

Replacing him is AO1 FEUILLERAT, alias the Rat, a name he received in his old attack squadron. It'll take a couple of months but we're all sure he'll come around soon.

Also among the new recruits are AO2 Terry HAND, AO2 James "Frizz" DAY, AO2 Robert "Andy" ANDERSON (our hero, who came to us after a year as a door gunner in Vietnam). Also we have AO3 Paul MASCOLINO "Moose" and our sweet thing AO3 Steven "Creep" KORBEL. They are all looking forward to their first WestPac Cruise and liberty in the Philippines.

Now to say a few words about the salts from the Chief JOHNSON era.

First off, our division officer, ITJG Dave CARPOWICH, the "Head Polack". After last cruise, Mr. C. has learned the tricks of the trade and can pick up the trail of a beer two days out of port. A hidden quality of Mr. "C" that few people know: he seconds as a conductor and serenades the ready room with the Rat Pack to the popular tunes of "Musical Missiles" (in B minor) "The Cap Condition Suite" and our old favorite, "The Ballad of the Wing Pylon".

-11-

AO3 Jim COTTON, "J.C.", just celebrated his 3rd anniversary in the VF-194 Ordnance Shop last week. If you see him in the passageways, just ask him about all his glorious memories. He has somehow with the use of his magical powers persuade the Rat to let him have the beach detachment.

Along with "J.C." is AO3 Louis FUSSELL "Inca". He also has been in VF-194 close to three years. Many people think of him as a very quiet and shy individual. But his knowledge of the ordnanceman's responsibilities is devastating and every now and then he releases his knowledge to us all.

Then, of course, there is AO3 Donald KIMBALL "Skafoso". He hails from Boston and brings the true italian accent to the shops. As soon as the word secure comes to the shop, he is the first to grab his pen and paper to write his wife and young daughter. He is also engaged as production directed of the first "Rat Pack", soon to be showing a theaters everywher.

Another of last year's old timers is AO3 Bruce HAKANSON "Hank"? "Sheep Herder", or "Short Ribs". Bruce is expecting an early discharge to go back to the ranch. Lately, he's been practicing herding the "Rat Pack" around the flight deck. Unfortunately to no avail. He is been complaining about the stray in the chow hall and island. Due to the lack of his horse (though he has tried to take it aboard) he constantly sticks his into the "Rat". Anyone having cats aboard contact him at Extension 624. When he leaves we'll be looking for a new recreation P.O.

Last but not least we have AO3 Lawrence Waulilet "Wally". Two finer points are, he always seems to be the first in the chow line and is the current star o of "Rat Pack" Productions. He is also leading in the shop masttache growing contest, primarily because of a two week head start. Wally comes from Wisconsin and his intake of milk is second only to his intake of beer.

As you can see with this crew a good cruise is forth coming, all ordnanse systems up and ordnancemen down.

After an enjoyable time is Hawaii, we're all looking forward to a fine reunion with old San Miguel in the Philippines. We'll try to keep you posted on coming events for the "Rat Pack" in the next edition of the Red Lightning Illustrated. We hope to have pictures in the near future. Keep the mail coming, we're all looking forward to our December homecoming!

-12-

Animal Talk

ADJ3 R. L. "Fat Al" ALLEN

Yes sir, folks of our fan club, here we are again back for a nice south seas cruise upon the Mighty "O". The story is still the same but some faces have changed to fill in for those that ever set free or have moved to another location.

The person who is leader of the following highly coordinated disastor is the one and only John ROCKWELL III Fighter Pilot, U.S.N. (at least thats what his name tag says.) Better known to us as (Rocky Sir) his two under studies are Chief SCOTT who we call Chief and Ronald FLINN with the side name of Ronald McDONALD. For a back up crew of new personal we have Terry MILROY (Mil Nips) Paul SAMANIE (Grit) Dave LANTZ (Lantzer) Mike STRAWBRIDGE (Strawberry) Rod RAYMOND (Rod) Armando PEREZ, who has a very short title of (Armando, Remondo, Garcia, Peres) and yours truly (Fat Albert) Richard Luckey ALLEN.

Of course we can't forget the oldies but goodies. Mark WESELY starts off the list known as (Big Face) B. A. SMITH is next! 69 days to go. Name: (Smitty). There is also Dave JEWELL (Boober) Shawn GUINN (Shawn Burger) Tom WALDEN (Ace) Lawrence THOMPSON (Toby) Mike WHITE (The Honorable Judge Uncle Mike) Dave PEACOCK (Mississippi) Stephen SENSNEY (Senseless) Lee Ray GRAY (Tha Did) Thomas DOYLE (Young Tom) E. G. NELSON (Shark) Fred IHRKE (Manomen MaiA), G. L. BRYAN (Pig Pen) S. L. FRAGAPANE (Puss). It is said no one could ever possess a mug like that and yet be for real. Larry SCHULING (Lawrence of Poland) is last but not least on the list.

Favorite sayings of the line crew this year are "Oh Yeaaa", "Wrong again" and "We love it". Our songs are the "Come on We're All Going to Die" Rag and "Born to Lose".

Just about everyone has had their yearly flight deck injury and all is proceeding normally. There has been a new feature added this year. That is, to make known to all by awarding each month to one of our pilots who has shown outstanding qualities in trying to better officer and enlisted relations, a letter of commendation, honorary plane captain's jersey and several other goodies. This award is not taken lightly by the line crew and the recipient of this is highly looked upon and given the highest respect.

-13-

Last month the winner of this award was LTJG Rod PARKER. Congratulations, Mr. PARKER, our zinger-bringing hero! This month's award has not been presented because of the vast amount of names submitted. However, as soon as the review board convenes, we will make known the winner. So, keep a sharp eye on the next Line Animals.

Speaking for the whole line crew, "We love you girls and keep the mail coming!"

Keep smiling, Mr. ERMIS, we're already confused!

-14-

You can relax
now, Mr. PHANEUF.
We've already taken
the picture!

The RED LIGHTNING ILLUSTRATED is published periodically by the Legendary Red Lightnings of Fighter Squadron ONE HUNDRED NINETY FOUR and is a product of the Public Affairs Office in conjunction with the Admin Office.

ADVISOR: LT J. C. JOHNSON
EDITOR: YN2 David K. BOWMAN
ASS'T EDITOR: AO2 T. L. SAND
STAFF ARTIST: ATN2 Gary L. McKISSICK
TYPIST: SN Cris CRISTOBAL

CONTRIBUTORS

LT Rocky ROCKWELL   AZ2 Andy RONQUILLO
AO3 Larry MAUTLET   ADJ3 R. L. ALLEN

Volume II   Number 1   JUNE 1970   A RED LIGHTNING PUBLICATION

SKIPPER

On assuming command of Fighter Squadron ONE HUNDRED NINETY FOUR, I cannot help but think of our men who are giving of themselves for their country, while malcontents continue to create unstable conditions back home. I can assure all of you parents, wives, sweethearts, brothers, sisters, sons, daughters and friends that these fine men are doing an outstanding job. Life is not easy aboard an aircraft carrier. The heat is at times unbearable and working hours are long and grueling. I am continually amazed at how well they perform and keep their sense of humor during these most arduous conditions. One might ask himself, what is their reward? The answer is simple — a sense of pride. Whether in for a short term or a career, they will have gained self-respect and won the admiration of all those citizens who really know what it's all about.

James W. RYAN
Commander
United States Navy
Commanding Officer

PROLOGUE

Due to circumstances beyond our control, this issue of
The RED LIGHTNING ILLUSTRATED was a bit late off the press.
To make up for this inconvenience, the staff has put together
an extra long issue full of juicy articles from both July
and August.

For the last three weeks the Red Flashes spent eight
days resting in Cubi Point and now we find ourselves deep
in a hard 22 day line period on Yankee Station.

J. C. JOHNSON
Lieutenant (junior grade)
United States Navy
RLI Advisor

ATTEN-SHUN!

HUD'N HUD'N CHANGE OF COMMAND

On Thursday, 2 July 1970, the command of Fighter Squadron ONE HUNDRED NINETY FOUR passed from Commander Joseph VINTI to Commander James RYAN. At 1000 all hands fell into ranks and came to attention for the ceremonies. Soon the guests of honor arrived, falling in behind the podium in order—CAPT GILICRIST, RADM RAMAGE, CDR CARLSON, CDR VINTI, CDR RYAN and Chaplain GATELY. Chaplain GATELY gave a brief Benediction and the Change of Command commenced. The Guest of Honor, Rear Admiral RAMAGE addressed the assembly first. Then, the Commander of the Troops reported all hands present and ready for inspection. The inspection party proceeded and returned to the podium where the final portion of the ceremony took place. The ceremony concluded when Commander RYAN stepped firmly forward, saluted Commander VINTI and said "I relieve you, sir." Immediately following the ceremony, a reception was held for the officers and guests at the Cubi Point Officers' Club. (See pictures on the next three pages)

-1-

The Maintenance Good Guys

WEST PAC '70

By LTJG J. C. JOHNSON

For the last part of July, we of Red Lightnings find ourselves finishing up an eight day second line period on Yankee Station and anticipating our return to Cubi Point. For the period of this issue of The Red Lightning Illustrated we completed a very successful first line period and enjoyed ten days rest at Cubi Pt. Before returning to the rigors of Yankee Station.

Our first line period was a very satisfying and gratifying experience. Everyone in our organization was full of spirit and excitement and many "HUD'N HUD'NS" were heard about the ship as personnel went about the business of maintaining and flying The Red Flash Birds. Maintenance did a superb job of keeping our aircraft up and in excellent condition. Maintenance was so good that many pilots were hard put to find that "Something" wrong for the midnight launch. This fact led to a good many flight hours for The Red Flashes.

For the first two days in Cubi preparations were in full swing for VF-194's change of command. It was the 2nd of July 1970 that we said good-bye to our skipper, Commander Joe VINTI, and welcomed to the helm - Commander Jim RYAN. More about the change in our feature article for this issue.

Anyone who was unaware of the meaning of "Monsoon" must surely know by now. It seemed as though the Philippine Islands were under water for the first five days of our inport period. However, rain was never a reason to deter Red Flashes from having a good time while in port. Grande Island was a familiar haven for many, as well as the golf course, beaches, and other recreational facilities around Cubi Pt. and Naval Station Subic. A few of us made the trip to Manila.

The rain did no favors for our F-8's however, and maintenance had its hands full trying to dry them out. It took a lot of oil on the afterburner eyelids and many test hops before the aircraft were ready for our second line period. However, we had a successful fly out to the ship from Cubi and an uneventful transit to Yankee Station.

Now we look forward to a successful completion to our second line period and our third in port period in Cubi.

—5—

141

From the Ready Room

The time is midnight. The place is Ready Room Five aboard the USS ORISKANY. Ready Room Five is the home of fifteen fighter pilots who call themselves "Red Flashes" and have an enviable reputation for themselves among their peer group of naval aviators. The Ready Room is unusually quiet this evening. Perhaps it's the beginning of the midnight 'till noon workday or perhaps it's because the few who are up and about are the duty officer and the pilots who are going out on the night launch. The duty officer this morning is Rod PARKER and presently he and Don PRIEST are engaged in a cribbage duel that may last several more hours. For Rod it helps pass the time 'till he can shirk his rather unenviable title of duty officer. Don is here, although he does not fly for several hours. This would be a logical time for Don to sleep, but his physiology has succumbed to the rather confusing and inconsistent stimuli that this work environment presents. One day we are working noon to midnight; twenty-four hours later we are on a midnight to noon schedule. Our bodies are reluctant conformers to this new schedule. They desire to sleep about the time we are catapulted off the bow of this iron behemoth; they yearn for activity when we know they should be getting sleep in preparation for the coming day. Meals are equally confusing. When going to the wardroom, we find a breakfast menu while our intuition has convinced us that roast beef and potatoes would have been more appropriate. The most consistent portion of this environment is possibly its lack of predictability.

Yes, the ready room is quiet now, but in a few short hours, the tempo will quicken. The room will fill with pilots briefing for their next flight. A few fortunates will come, having just arisen from a full night's sleep. The air is filled with the friendly but often cutting satire that makes up the ready room dialogue. The most tense moments are those when all eyes are glued to a small television screen in one corner of the room. We are watching our buddies make their landings. These are critical moments and they are vicarious experiences for every pilot who watches. Each of us are making men mental corrections for the approach we see one of our buddies make. At night, the tension is especially high until all our birds are again safely nestled on the ORISKANY's deck. The conversation and atmosphere is unusually jovial and light-hearted as the returning pilots enter the ready room. The joy of a safe recovery overshadows any remaining tension left from the hop. After a night recovery the pilots are joking and slapping each other playfully on the back like a group of high school boys. Although their happiness is real, they are not high school boys. They are men who have successfully completed a task requiring training, skill and composure. Much of the flight demanded intense concentration -- equally as intense is their relief.

-6-

142

Even though there are moments of loneliness for the family and friends stateside, the time still manages to pass quickly. Although we wish the cruise was completed, we are relieved to realize it is at least one third over. The remainder of the summer must expire, autumn come and go, and winter begin before we are united with our families again. We try not to think of this often, for it lengthens moments that would have otherwise passed quickly.

"Hey Jock! Time to brief for your hop!"

"Just a second, Rod. Let me finish this article."

"You're a little late as it is, Jock. Better get going."

"- - Okay, Okay!"

* * * * * * * * * * * * * * * * * * * *

HID'N HUD'N CHIEFS - From left to right, top row, AEC DAVIS, ATCS JORGENSON (LCPO), AMHC SCOTT, ATC BONNER, AQC HATHCOCK; left to right, front row, ADCS HEILAND, ATC HAM-MARLUND and AOC GREENE. Not shown was PNC CRISTOBAL who was on re-enlistment leave.

-7-

143

OUR INNKEEPERS

One group of people no one evers considers as having an essential job are the squadron compartment cleaners. Their job is very important to the health and well being of squadron personnel. They devote there time to cleaning the compartment every morning and always making sure the ship's instruction on cleaning is met everyday.

The squadron's P.P.O. is a man of great knowledge. He has to know how to repair and evaluate any emergency which may arise. Tiny Jim is his name but known better to most of us as "Boots" (BM3 RUCH). He came to the squadron from Japan and is thinking of extending for the cruise. He has been doing a fine job and are proud to have him on our team.

Our compartment cleaners are young men with great respect for the Naval service. Senior man in this division is T.I. (AN NELSON), who has been with the squadron for three years now. During this last import he spend most of his free time diving for many sea articles. Our second young man is known as "Boot Camp #1". He is from Texas and a great Beatla fan. Boot Camp #1 (AMHAN MAHAN) spend most of his time this last import studying the different customs of the Filipino people. Our third is know as "Boot Camp #2". He is also from the state of Texas. Boot Camp #2 (SN BARBEE) is no doll. Before he came in the Navy someone told him he would get a head and he did. The forth and last is the great philosopher and lives by his teachings. Sholty will make a great airman whenever he makes it.

To all of our compartment cleaners from the guys in the squadron a very warm thank you.

-8-

144

KN@W Y@UR LINE ANIMALS

By LT Rocky ROCKWELL

Anyone who is a Bill Cosby fan should certainly be familiar with the childhood character made famous in his routines, known as Fat Albert. When he walks, the sidewalk shakes and his fantastic size and weight made it possible for his neighborhood to have Philadelphia's champion "Buck-Buck" team. We of the Legendary Red Lightnings are fortunate in having our own resident "Fat Albert," a 22-year-old troubleshooter named Richard Lucky ALLEN. Tipping the scales at perhaps just a skosh under the combined weight of the other 5 troubleshooters (minus their tool belts), Allen sometimes seems to make the flight deck rumble a bit when he moves around on it changing tires, and of course his presence on the line has certainly been a great help in making VF-194's Maintenance Department one of the best in the Pacific Fleet.

Al comes from a small town in Maryland called Noinsville, about 45 miles north of Baltimore, whose population is hovering around the "century" mark. After graduation from North Hartford High School in 1966, he worked for a few months, then joined the "Nav" in February 1967, doing his boot camp at the Great Lakes Naval Training Center. From there he went to Jet Mechanic "A" school in Memphis, then spent a few weeks TAD with VF-124 and joined the Red Lightnings in December 1967, just in time to make the 1968 WestPac cruise.

During the 1969-70 turnaround, Al managed to get 30 days leave to go home and get married, and now he and his wife are expecting a little ADJ next January.

While in VF-194 Allen made ADJ3, and he has worked in the Power Plants shop as well as the line. His main duties as a troubleshooter comprise changing tires and servicing the hydraulic and pneumatic systems on our F-8 crusaders.

When his enlistment is up in February 1971, Allen plans to go back to school with a view toward getting his FAA Power Plants and Airframes certificate so he can work as a mechanic on civilian aircraft (most of which are a little easier to maintain than the F-8).

In his spare time Al likes to hunt birds and small game and dabble in auto repairs. When he was in high school he played saxophone in the school band. One of the highlights of his movied career was when the school band went to the New York World's Fair in 1964 and played at the different pavilions.

"Fat Albert" ALLEN's hard work, dedication to duty and good sense of humor have made him an indispensable mechanic and petty officer, as well as a fine example and friend to all who have known and worked with him.

* * * * * * * * * * * * * * * * * * * *

The Red Lightnings latest Plane Captain of the month, for the month of May, is a tall, slender AE3 by the name of Lee Ray GRAY, better known to his fellow Line Animals ad squadron notes as "The Kid." GRAY did such an outstanding job as a Plane Captain back at Miramar that he was selected by his supervisors to be the lucky plane captain to fly to Hawaii as part of the beach detachment before and during our Operational Readiness Evolution, rather than riding the ship over. Since rejoining the squadron after the ORE he has consistently made his aircraft, NM 203, stand out as one of the cleanest and best cared for in the Air Wing.

"The Kid" comes from Morehead City, North Carolina, where he played offensive and defensive end on West Carteret High School's Eastern Conference Championship football team. Not exactly what you'd call a bench warmer, he modestly recalls being selected the team's most outstanding player of the year, a feat made even more significant by the fact that he was the smallest member of the team at 150 pounds wringing wet.

After graduation in 1968 Lee went right into the Navy, doing his boot camp at Great Lakes. From there, he went to AE "A" School in Jacksonville, did the usual TAD tour with VF-124 at Miramar, then joined the Red Lightnings last August in the middle of our cruise.

Although GRAY's father is one of the finest auto mechanics in the state of North Carolina, Lee's ambition lies in another direction. After separation from the Navy in August of 1972, he hopes to go to college, possibly North Carolina State, and study to become a high school history teacher. He presently plans to settle down back in North Carolina.

Between WestPac cruises, GRAY likes to spend his spare time surfing, fishing and water skiing. While he was in high school, he worked for two years in a butcher shop, but would just as soon not go back to that now (even though it must be easier than carrying chain bags on the flight deck). His second choice for a career, he informs us, is to be some sort of electrician (civilian, that is).

One final note: After returning from a hop the other day, our new XO, CDR METZLER, commented that his canopy, which GRAY had cleaned as a part of his pre-flight, was the "cleanest F8 canopy line I've seen in my naval career." This is no mean praise coming from a man with over 1500 hours in F8 Crusaders.

LTJG Dave CARPOWICH mans the duty desk.

-10-

146

AO1 Bob "Rat" FEUILLERAT examines
ordnance attached to F8 Crusader

ADJ3 Rick "Fat Albert" ALLEN on
the job (see article on page 9)

-11-

147

Greetings from the **RAT·PAC**

By AO3 Larry WAUTLET

Once again the fighting ordies of VF-194 are about to come through with another article for the Red Lightning Illustrated.

First we want to say "hi" to all the wives, parents, children girl friends and friends for the numerous letters, post cards and packages that have been sent to us the past month. Keep up the good work, everyone is a lot easier to work with after a mail call.

Since our last edition, we have acquired a new chief. His name is Chief Roy GREENE. He comes from Colorado and seems to be fitting into the shop very well. He's come up with some new ideas which make work a bit easier and liberty more enjoyable for us all.

There have been a few changes in shop assignments since our last article. Bruce "Hank" HAKANSON has finally bid us farewell and by now should be reading this article from an easy chair back home in North Dakota. We all wish you the best of luck, Bruce, in your new job.

James "J.C." COTTON has, very happily, after a month of beach detachment, come back to the confines of the ship. Everything seems to be going very well with "J.C." now that he is out to sea again. He and Paul "Moose" MASCOLINO have taken over night check maintenance. They have formed their own secret organization of the "Molly Maguires". Some guys see one movie in port and they don't forget it the whole line period. Oh well, they're happy and they do get the job done quite well.

Once again, as the ship nears the end of another line period, we are about to lose another of our long time friends and fellow ordnancemen. Yes, friends, Louis F. FUSSELL "Luca" has received orders and is moving his residence to NAS Oceana, Virginia. We're all going to miss you Lou. "Rat" AO1 Robert FEUILLERAT have been holding secret meetings with "Luca", to make sure he gets all of the vast ordnance knowledge Lou has acquired in VF-194.

-12-

Before I go any further, I must inform you that the weight losing contest between "Rat" and AO2 Terry HAND is still under way. "Rat" claims to have lost the most, but if you talk to Terry, he says he's way ahead. They both still have a few extra pounds to go, but they're working hard at it. Our parachute rigger moved out of the ordnance shop because he ran out of material to make thermal belts for the both of them.

As you all probably know by now, the Legendary Red Lightnings have a new man at the helm. Change of command ceremonies were held in the Philippines last time in port. Commander Jim RYAN took over from Commander Joe VINTI. The new skipper has already made the fatal mistake of challenging the enlisted personnel to a volley ball and softball tournament this time in port. We also have a squadron party planned for the in port period. It should give everyone a little chance to let off steam and relax a bit before the long line period coming up in August.

AO3 Steve KORBEL "Commander" is now running the flight deck during the day. Seems a few of the guys were having a little trouble with the ordnance system on a plane one day. Steve politely told them to go down to the shop and stay out of his way. He said he'd handle the launch and I guess he did pretty well. He has since acquired the nick name of "commander". Even the "Rat" stays out of his way now.

AO3 Donald KIMBALL, AO2 Robert ANDERSON, AO2 James Day and AO3 Lawrence WAUTLET are still around. Don "Shefoss" KIMBALL still writes home every day and leads the shop as usual in receiving mail. Although the Chief, "Moose" MASCOLINO and "Fritz" DAY are running close second.

"Andy" is adjusted pretty well to F-8 fighter ordnance. He still has everyone's attention when he tells one of his combat stories about Vietnam, however. He's a good guy and gets along well with all the fellas.

L. "Wally" WAUTLET is still in mourning over the loss of his good buddy Bruce "Hank" HAKANSON. San Miguel lost a good customer when Bruce left, so Wally's trying to keep up for the both of them.

LTJG GARPOWICH, "Mister C." has got the whole shop really confused. We though we had gotten him on the right deck jersey. Then he turns around and puts on a "Canary Yellow" jersey. I guess we'll have to get back down in the ordnance shop and get him "squared away".

Everything has gone as well as can be expected so far this cruise. We all miss our loved ones back in the United States. Keep up the letters, folks. The time between mail calls seems very long. The few minutes you may spend writing is worth many hours of pleasure to the guys over here. Keep up the good work.

December is coming and if we can keep our spirits light and the line periods short, I'm sure we'll all make it home safely and broke. The coming events include another nine days of the Philippines and our longest line period of the cruise so far.   Until next month I'll sign off.

-13-

149

A TRIP DOWN
SOUTH

By
LT Rod PARKER

On July 3, immediately following VF-194's change of command two of The
Red Flash pilots embarked on a trip to Zamboanga City, on the island of
Mindanao.

Getting there proved to be half the fun. LT Don WALLIS and LTjg Rod
PARKER sniveled a hop from Cubi Pt. to Clark, AFB. There they talked their
way into a flight going to the Southern Philippines carrying everything from
an X-Ray machine to several cases of San Miguel beer. At a field called
Cagayan De Oio (place of gold) somewhere in the islands the C-47, "gooney
bird," landed for some unknown reason. By coincidence Philippine Air Lines
had a flight directly to Zamboanga within the next 15 minutes. A switch
was hastely executed and the two travelers found themselves at their dest-
ination just about 24 hours after the adventure began.

Zamboanga, a city of about 17,000, is located at the very Southern tip
of Mindanao, about 600 miles from Subic Bay. It's a very pleasant city in
that no commercialization exists such as in Olongapo and Manila. The people
there were extremely friendly and courteous so making friends was easy.
Another nice feature was the prices of everything. With no tourists to speak
of the economy is geared to the populace consequently we ended up spending
considerably less than if we had stayed at Cubi.

The main livelyhood seems to fishing, but at times jeepney or tricycle
driving also appears to be a prominant profession. One of the other "industries"
in Zamboanga is the collection, distribution, and sale of sea shells. On
almost every corner there are people with small displays of shells they offer
for almost nothing. Since this area is just about the best in the world for
sea shells there are also some large world-wide distributors and shell shops
located in the city.

Although one could buy nearly any type of shell desired at a fraction of
its stateside value here we decided to find our own. Most of the four days
we were there were spent diving along the coral reefs and islands that lie
all around the city. Each morning, as the sun came up, two of the local
fisherman would come by our hotel in their boat to pick us up. Some of the
most fun occured when talking to the men while riding to and from the diving
areas.

One of the surprising thing we learned was that most of the people in the area
are Moslems. Another was that they considered in both to be between 35 and 40
years old and wealthy beyond description! To be considered rich wasn't too
bad, but being put in the some age category as Major ERMIS was beyond our
comprehension.

-14-

150

One thing's for sure. The trip really whetted our appetite for another to the same area. I think we may also have inspired some of the other squadrons pilots to give Zamboanga a try.

LT Don PRIEST shakes hands with CAPT GILLCRIST at a recent cake cutting ceremony celebrating LT PRIEST's 155,000th Arrested Landing aboard USS ORISKANY. LT PRIEST was awarded an engraved cigarette lighter along with the cake. Also pictured, far right, is CDR C.D. METZLER, VF-194's XO.

-15-

151

David K. Bowman

Super Tuners & Metal Manglers

ADJ1 R. W. EVANS

Stuck away in a far away corner of the USS ORISKANY near a ladder Compartment C-115-A may sometime look like a Swap Shop or a California Card Room, Air Conditioned no less, but to those who haven't stepped through the threshold they can not fully understand what goes on behind our brite Orange and Pea Green Door_____ which was dedicated this cruise to our most Illusive Metalsmith "WILLIE" (AMH3 WILLIAMS).

Under the cracking black whip of LT. "Jock" WALLIS, hand-in-hand, the Power Plants and Air Frames Shops keep the old F8s flying only things new about it are what we put in it: engine parts, oil, hydraulic fluid and lines_____sometimes new metal.

But without these two shops keeping the planes turning and burning we would not be living up to our name "THE RED LIGHTNINGS."

Between assisting shops with gripes and our work, the below listed personnel have shown everyone that they are Professionals in all respect.

POWERPLANTS

ADJ1 "BIG BOB" Evans (Day Supervisor)
ADJ3 "Be the Birdman" Bohannon
ADJ3 "Mike" Pedersen
ADJ3 "Willy" Gray
ADJ3 "Chuck" Quale
ADJ3 "Goat" Goedacke
ADJ3 "Duck" Duax
ADJ2 "Crudley" Crumly (Nite Supervisor)
ADJ2 "Great" Dain (New Addition to Power Plants)

AIR FRAMES

AMH1 "Do me a favor" JENNINGS (Day Supervisor)
AMH1 "TJ" Hunt (Nite Supervisor)
AMS2 "Scotch-Weld" Sanders
AMS2 "Little Jon" Johnson
AMH2 "Uncle Vernie" Maulding
AMS2 "Mike" Tell (New Addition to AirFrames)
AMH3 "Rick" Rickwald
AMH3 "Red" Jordan
ADJ3 "Dupree and AMH3 Williams TAD to Ship
AMSAN "Chip" Grimes

-16-

152

"LINE ANIMALS"

BY THE LINE BEAN

Dearly Beloved, we are gathered here again to bring forth this months laughs and sorrows of our second line period.

Though some what of a short line period we are experiencing a different atmosphere. We've purchased a tape recorder and now our line dances to another tune.

We are a group of individuals as is shown by our music. We vary in music as do our sizes and personalities. From Acid Rock to Soul and from Jazz to Country Western. You can create a riot merely by changing a tape. Without individualism it would be all sorrow for the line.

The Grit is one great example of individualism. "Ax me any question, if I don't know the answer I'll argue the issue anyhow".

Our line crew consist of a group of young men. These men have been drawn together for a common purpose. Pulling last minute maintenance and sending our pilots out. However when day is done our community does not desintergrate. We're a family. We eat, sleep, morn, and celebrate together. We laugh at each other and we stand up for each other when the time arises.

Let it be known that even though the pilots are now jogging from their planes to the ready room we have no fear. For we are in shape, to accept challenge in any sport they would care to select. From Volleyball, Softball to three legged races. We will accept the challenges on the (23rd or 24th) at Dungaree Beach. We feel such an event as the squadron picnic should prove to increase our thirst and hunger.

Irish DOYLE and Face WESELY are still trying to learn how to play pinockle and will greatly appreciate any suggestions offered. They have greatly improved however, they've now won eleven of fifty one games played.

Some of the guys will be leaving the line soon to become civilians again. B.A. SMITH tells us every day how short he's getting while others like "Shark" NELSON just smile as days pass. There are many more leaving while on this cruise and we'll miss all of them. But as one leaves another takes his place and life continues on the line.

The recepiant of the June award for Honarary Plane Captain is LT John H. ROCKWELL,III. As was stated in the awards ceremony by the honorable judge Uncle Mike "His efforts and success in creating a better enlisted-officer relation won LT ROCKWELL this award.

Our heartiest congratulations go to LT ROCKWELL. In closing there are a few last minute notes. Shawn GUINN has injured his right shoulder muscle. He will be out of work for a few weeks and we miss his presence on the flight deck. Pig Pen has a new friend-a pocket ben. It ticks so loudly it keeps half the compartment awake.

Congradulation to the following men: Michael STRAWBRIDGE (Strawberry) advancement to AMS3, Lawrence THOMPSON (Toby) advancement to AMS3, Lee R. GRAY (The Kid) plane captain for the month of May.

-17-

OUR GANG

BY

AZ2 ANDY RONQUILLO

Cubi Pt. has become to most of us our second home. Being that we are inport at least one week each month, it has been a common sight for VF-194. During our last inport we had the pleasure of celebrating our Independance Day in Cubi Pt. Norb the Great (ADCS HEILAND), Curly (ADJC DIAMOND) and Snoopy (AEC DAVIS) spend their nights at the Cubi CPO Club. Bonnie of Clyde (AZC BONNER) was out doing his duty be enjoying himself while standing his shore patrol. Many of the men won't forget him due to the fact he brought us back one way or the other. HUD'N HUD'N! For this he was awarded the "Good Guy Award".

Snoopy (AEC DAVIS) will be leaving us in the middle of August to Norfolk, Va. We will all miss him for the great job he has done for the squadron.

Curly (ADJC DIAMOND) is still trying to learn how to play the banjo and the song his son was trying to teach him while he was home. I hope by the time he get home again he will be able to play that song. As for the others in our shop go, they have all had a good time this inport. Fred FARRELL Farkel (AK1 FARRELL), Chilly T (AK2 TORRES) and the Frito Bandido (AZ2 RONQUILLO) spend most of their time at the Acey Duey Club. Chilly T and the Frito Bandido were invited by NIS (AKC CUIZON) to his sisters house and had a very good time. Blue Jackets (AMH CARR) was either on the ship or on shore patrol. Chester (AZ3 DILLON) was busy studying the Filipino customs and Mur the Surf (ADJAN MURPHY) was in Manila on a tour. Tex (AN EPPS) and Mustang Mush (ATN3 McKISSICK) were having a contest to see who could sleep the longest.

We are happy to introduce to you our new member to our Maint/Cont. family. His name is Lew (AZ3 LEWIS) and is very happy to be in our organization. So here is to you Lew, a warm welcome aboard and HUDN HUDN.

We are also very happy to announce to the world that Bonnie of Clyde (AZC BONNER) has been made Maintenance Control Chief. Good Luck.

This is for Blue Jackets family, please keep on sending the candy we all like it. As the weeks go by I will try to keep you informed on the activities of our fine squadron and the men that make it. Adios to all of you and good night "Big Dick" wherever you are.

-18-

154

PR1 ROGER RAMJET FLINN

We're still around the Mighty "C", guys. If you are still looking for us, good luck. We move pretty fast.

We would like to thank LT D.A. WALLIS for all the help he has given the shop during his tour as Aircraft Division Officer. We wish him good luck in his new job as NATOPS/Training Officer.

Also, we would like to welcome LT W. C. DURHAM to the Aircraft Division as our new Division Officer. Yes sir, this is your lucky day. The VF-194 PR's, Inc. belong to you. We're formally known as work center 130 in case someone should ask. We're looking forward to seeing your signature on a few standard Navy forms...special liberty, leave...

We would like to thank the AME's for all the help they have given us. Keep it up, guys. We can use all the help we can get.

We're all looking forward to the Squadron Picnic our next time in port. We feel the PR's, with a little help from the rest of the Aircraft Division, will take all honors in the sports competition—we may be few but we're effective.

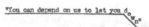

"You can depend on us to let you down"

PR3 LOIS IAIN

Believe it or not! Yes, we do have a Parachute Rigger operating in the squadron. There are four of us actually; Ron FLY PR1 is our official shop supervisor. Donald CLARK PR2 who's been with us since February, myself, PR3 Joel IAIN, and PRAN Mike ABEL, who reported in just a week or so ago.

FLINN has been acting as our squadron Line PO and has been devoting much of his time to that job. CLARK has been TAD since his arrival in the squadron and I am the operating PR in the squadron. Mike ABEL is my assistant. CLARK and I are due to change jobs soon. Good luck, Doni

Our Ordnancemen have been kind enough to accommodate our shop since the beginning of the cruise. It was only a couple days ago that we received our own space—behind the ready room. I'd like to personally thank the AO's at this time for assisting me and putting up with my little visit. But please take care of our little jewel of a sewing machine. You guys are all right.

On behalf of the squadron, our shop would like to thank the people at home for supporting us in our task by their letters and little goodies. Thank you.

-19-

"Who says life stops at 29?!"

A2C Mike BONNER caught recently by our photographer as he was participating in the CO's "Man of Steel" program of physical fitness.

"Alley Oop!"

AO2 HAND and AO3 KORBEL hefting a piece of ordnance.

-20-

Scope Dope

By Joe Muns AQF3

Throughout history every era has had its unsung heroes, and today is no exception. Within Fighter Squadron ONE NINE FOUR there are but a few such men. I am referring to the Fire Control Technicians of the Legendary AQ Shop. Day after day they perform their duties with never a thought to quitting. Their only reward is the satisfaction in the end result of their work. Their main concern is the upkeep of the radar. The F-8J aircraft is equipped with a highly complex and sophisticated radar capable of lock-on and tracking of any airborne target. Keeping every radar system in good working order is a 24 hours a day, 7 days a week job. Every technician must be tensively trained, so that when trouble arises he can quickly diagnose the problem which lies somewhere among the many thousand components throughout the system. His untiring efforts and high quality work is ever exemplified by the continual up status in radar equipment that VF-194 enjoys.

Apart from the normal shop activity nearly everyone has some sort of hobby or pastime.

James SHIFLER, commonly known as "R.L. Junior", is conducting a test on the ability of "HIS" chair to withstand rocking on its back legs. Since the return of Jimmie FOSTER to the shop "R.L. Junior" has had to take the #2 position in the shop, but he tries harder.

Wally "NO-SHRINK" BACON has lately been challenging for the shop coke drinking champion. Coming closer everyday to breaking the old record for cokes consumed in one day, 52, set by Fred STINSON on 23 June 1969. You can do it, Wally.

Jim SPECHT has not yet given up the notion that he can destroy A-7 bomb pylons with his head. His "hard headed" dedication makes him a top contender for sailor of the month.

Jeff "The Rudder" STRAND is one of our leading morale boosters. He has been referred to by many as the real night check supervisor.

Jerry GRUBBS, who digs on heavy sounds, is looking forward to getting back to his "Big G" ranch in Texas, in the not too distant future. (That is if Chief HATHCOCK doesn't ship him over first).

Rumor has it that Jimmie FOSTER has been trying to go TAD to A/F-F/P for some time now. One of his favorite pastimes as well as SHIFLER's is bragging about how VW's handle like sports cars.

We hear that Ron WILSON is thinking of having a certain piece of sidewalk bronzed(?) Ron has the unique ability to change his appearance at will by turning "RED".

-21-

157

Coming back was a little disappointing. After leading a somewhat idyllic life for a few days adjusting to the normal Navy routine was a little unsettling.

Last but not least we have Roland "LUIGI" JAWORSKI, the only Jewish, Italian, Pollock in the world! He's a real hustler and has the knack of getting the job done when the chips are down.

It is not likely that there ever has been nor ever will be another group of men such as these.

AE3 Lee R. GRAY, a recent Plane Captain of the Month.

-22-

158

SAILOR & P.C.
OF THE MONTH

Shown above are, left to right, BM3 James RUCH, AMS3 Thomas
WALDEN, CDR J. W. RYAN, the Commanding Officer, PR1 Ron FLYNN, and
AMS1 Charlie JOHNSON. They were photographed following an awards
ceremony held in late July at which BM3 RUCH was named Sailor of the
Month for July; AMS3 WALDEN was named Plane Captain of the Month for
June; and PR1 FLYNN and AMS1 JOHNSON recieved letters of commendation
for outstanding performance of duty.

-23-

R.L.I. STAFF

The Advisor   The Editor

The Staff Artist   The Staff Typist

The Assistant Editor →

The RED LIGHTNING ILLUSTRATED is published periodically by the
Legendary Red Lightnings of Fighter Squadron ONE HUNDRED NINETY
FOUR and is a product of the Public Affairs Office in conjunction
with the Admin Office.

STAFF		CONTRIBUTORS	
ADVISOR:	LTJG J.C. JOHNSON	CDR J.W. RYAN	AZ2 Andy RONQUILLO
EDITOR:	YN2 David K. BOWMAN	LT Jock WALLIS	PR3 Joel IAIN
ASS'T		LT Rocky ROCKWELL	AO3 Larry WAUTLET
EDITOR:	AC2 T.L. HAND	LTJG Rod PARKER	AE3 Terry MILROY
ARTIST:	ATN3 Gary L. MCKISSICK	ADJ1 R.W. EVANS	AQF3 Joe MUNZ
TYPIST:	SN Cris CRISTOBAL	PR1 Ron FLYNN	

Volume II Number 2 JULY-AUGUST 1970   A RED LIGHTNING PUBLICATION

-24-

September – October 1970

WEST PAC '70

By
LTJG Jon C. JOHNSON

This is the third RLI published this cruise and our fourth line period on Yankee Station. Since our last publication the Red Lightnings successfully completed our third line, then we joyfully steamed for Hong Kong where we enjoyed that magic city for 7 days. The weather in Hong Kong was exceptional which just might have enhanced our buying tendencies. I'm sure the Red Flashes did their share in increasing the wealth of camera and clothing merchants.

After Hong Kong it was back to Subic Bay to prepare for our forth line period. There was quite a bit of talk about a mid-cruise slump gripping VF-194. It seems that some squadrons start letting down and become discouraged about their work some where midway in a cruise. So far it is evident that the Red Flashes are just as enthusiastic about getting the job done and doing it right as they were at the beginning of the cruise. Perhaps the thought that this is our last long line period and that soon we will be returning home keeps us going.

The beginning of September saw a number of new personnel join our squadron. These include:

LT Dan Swenson, Assist. Maint. Off	ADJC Donald D. Wilbur
ABC Paul D. Sanders	ADJC Warren J. Fisher
AKAN George J. Tyson	AEAA Thomas J. Whaley
ATNAN John P. Collin	AKAN Peter R. Berg
AKAN Larry G. Beeney	

To all our new Red Flashes a hardy "Welcome Aboard". This will be the last issue by our proficient editor. YN2 BOWMAN is going the ways of a civilian at the end of this month. Editor BOWMAN's professionalism in putting together this newsletter will be greatly missed. We of the staff wish him the best of luck.

-1-

JENNINGS' RAIDERS

I know you have all heard of Jennings Raider. They are the Red Flash master minded hydraulic shop's beautiful people, alias metal manglers.

During this 1970 West Pac cruise, we are proud to have with us our most illusive metalsmith "Willy". As you go out on the job Willy is always there to keep you smiling and laughing, he is handing you wrenches and telling you stories.

Willy has been replaced this year by Boot Camp William Apple Tell AMS2. Then there are the Salty ones AMSAN Chip Grimes, Twinketoes Rickwald AMH3 and of course AMS2 Quink Sanders who by the way has 12,000 maintenance hours on the F-8 aircraft and still hasn't learned right from left.

Beware when you enter the threshold of the Jennings Raiders hang out because fast talking Jennings will have everything but your britches before you know it. Jennings Raiders are headed up by LT Bull Durham and Chief Bighorn Hudson. During this line period Jennings Raiders have recieved many disturbing gripes but the final answer is usually in the Electric Shop (Hi Fred).

The "Beautiful People" of the master minded hydraulic shop have done a great job keeping the old F-8 fighter flying. And also with the help of our last but not least career designated night check: HUNT AME1, JOHNSON AMS2, MAULDING AMH2, JORDAN AMH3.

Written by: SANDY AMS2 and RICK AMH3

-2-

-5-

SAILOR & P.C.
OF THE MONTH

At a late Aug. Ceremony shown above are the Sailor of the Month for July, AK2
Mario S. TORRES, (Second from the left) and Plane Captain of the month for July,
AN Don LANTZ (second from right) with the Commanding Officer, CDR J.W. RYAN.
also shown are ATC N.V. JORGENSON, far left; AOC Robert HATHCOCK, far right; and
AK1 P.D. FARRELL, next to AOC HATHCOCK; all of whom recieved Armed Forces Good
Conduct Metels.

-6-

AME1 R.A. NELSON pictured above with CDR J.W. RYAN, HUD'N HUD'N CO, shortly after he reenlisted for 4 years.

AT1 David COPELAND reenlists for 6 years.

-7-

Greetings from the RAT·PAC

By AO3 Larry WAUTLET

Again time has come for another entree in the logs of the famous Red Lightning Ordnance Shop.

Presently we are in port, Hong Kong. As I write this article, Don Kimball and myself are sitting in front of a tall, cool, glass of spirits. We've been running up and down the streets, getting in our last few days of shopping. Everyone is quite tired out, checking bargains and prices from different tailors, and stuffing themselves with all the fabulous oriental food. Just trying to cram so much, into so few days is awful hard to accomplish.

I would imagine there will be a lot said about Hong Kong in this edition of the Red Lightning Illustrated. Still, I must include a few words about the exploits of the ordies, while here.

Paul Mascolino and "Frity" Day have been on picture taking excursions all around the ship with all of his lenses, filters and film hung around his neck. You know its more than just a hobby for him.

All of the guys have brought many gifts and articles for their wives and families. I don't want to mention any of the items in this article, it may spoil a lot of surprises back home.

I must say though, Kodak will never go out business as long as 194's ordies are in port. There will be many an afternoon spent with our loved ones, showing pictures and telling stories of all the great times we had, while touring these far east ports.

Although we are all having a good time here, we are here in body only, our minds and hearts are back home with all of you. We still can't wait until that seemingly far off day in December, when we'll be coming home to you all.

Mr. Carpowich's pretty wife, journeyed to Hong Kong with many of the other wives, making the stay much more enjoyable for those lucky few. I am sure he's having a great time. We won't know until the ship pulls out, because he's been no where insight for the past few days.

-8-

Rat and the ^Chief have fallen in line with the rest of the camera bugs. I met Chief Greene yesterday on the street. I saw this huge bundle of packages moving along and walked over for a better look, sure enough. It was the chief with bargains.

Don Kimball and I ran into Rat today. We walked around a corner and ran right into a 300 m.m. telephoto lens. Naturally, on the other end was Rat, with a great big smile on his face, having a great time.

Steve Kortel was in town yesterday also, I made the mistake of telling him about the great picture obtainable from Victoria Peak. So we journeyed, for my 3rd time, to the top of the peak. He shot two or three rolls of film and chatted with the local people for awhile. He could talk an Eskimo into a pair of water skis. He, as well, is having a good time in Hong Kong.

Robert Anderson has won the all time sleeping record for the ship. Being an old combat veteran of Viet Nam he still feels all these ports are a waste of time and effort. He believes all the problems of the world can be settled from your bed. If everyone is sleeping, there will be a lot less fighting. He gets this philosophy from smokey the Bear. Hibernation is the cure of all ills.

Donnie Kimball was just telling me about a really great meal he had yesterday. He says the escaeragots were a might oily, the ox tail soup was a bit thin, but the hamburgers were great. Some conniseurs of food. Give him the old hot dogs and hamburger and he's the most contented guy you've ever seen. Also, Don's birthday is coming up in early September. He will be, along with a couple other guys, getting out of the Navy upon our return to Alameda.

Our old and long gone friends Bruce Hakanson and Lore Fussell have been keeping in contact with us. Bruce is very happy on the ranch and is doing very well. In Loris last letter, he seems to like his new duty station in Virginia. We all wish you were back here with us. The shop is just not the same with out you guys.

Well, in a couple of days we'll be leaving P.I. once more. I'm sure I'm speaking for everyone, when I say we'll be glad to leave. It means we're that much closer to going home.

We have a big line period coming up after leaving the Philippines. The time seems to go much faster at sea when we're all working. Our last line period was the longest of the cruise thus far, and went quite well. We got our job kone in a very professional manner. Few people realize that if it wasn't for the ordnancemen, our mission here would be fruitless. Everyone gets along real well and with the help of our shop leaders Chief Roy Greene and Robert Feuillerat, it will continue that way. They have done an outstanding job thus far and I'm sure it will continue.

I always try to mention a little about each person in our shop. Seems I have forgotten three people thus far. Terry Hand, James Cotton, and Micheal Noonan. J.C. is The senior member of the shop, as he's been in 194 longer than anyone. If there is a gripe on a plane that no one can fix, we call on Jim and he takes control immediately. He will be leaving the Navy in a few months planning to go to college.

Mike Noonan just came into the shop last line period. This is his first chance to work in the shop since coming to 194 about nine months ago, He seems to fit in real well and all the guys like him alot.

-9-

FLIGHT
OPS

-10-

HUD'N HUD'N AE/AT SHOP

Story and picture by: AE3 Jeff WAGNER

Under the direction of Fearless Fred Kurzinger, we of the VR-194 AE-AT Shop have had many discussions covering the subjects of sports, food, liberty, books, people, various other sundry topics and of course, the steady flow of airplane troubles we are called upon so frequently to remedy as if by magic.

From the troubled aircraft to the trouble minds, we mix up our conversations to make a new dialogue. Since we all nkow what happened last turn around but not next, we speculate and find a new happiness in the word spoken with most pride--home--and we love you.

But that's not all we have. The daily quiz show, "Dumb for a Day", is one other. With all as judges, it's hard to say anything without someone saying "Give him a star". And just for saying something typical like "If someone doesn't dump the trash, there won't be any place to put it". Also various assorted programs such as the Physical Fitness Team, Sideburn and Hair Growing Team, Smoking Team, Soda Drinking Team and of course the Yelling Team. There was a recent survey held at which time it was decided that some people yell to feel fat, some to let out fat, and others to feel the yell build up inside and see it explode over everyone in the room. Fearless Fred is a well practiced yeller and surely the top in our shop. However, lately we have noticed that Mike Clay is working hard at getting the top spot before he gets out of the Navy in December. All in all, it is a good thing that the line period is over, as it has been noticed that more than a few of us have been losing our minds.

All in all, it is a good thing that the line period is over as it has been noticed that more than a few of us have been losing our minds.

Actually no record is kept of the out come of any of our contests, however, there is always a high rivalry in most cases, the reason being we suppose that the boredom would be more than unbearable if there weren't.

Mail call is a happy time here. Work stops for a few moments of chaos as the mail is sorted and read by us, the proud owners of people, friends and various other assorted relatives, who can share their far away lives and thoughts with us and at the same time remind us that those lives are still a very important part of our own lives and vise-versa, which is truly the key to communication of any kind. That "wanted" feeling gives us strength to carry on. And we love you for that.

Thank you and read this with the thought in mind that in time everyone will find a united peace.

-11-

KNOW YOUR LINE ANIMALS

By
Lt Rocky ROCKWELL

As the Red Flash pilots wander around the flight deck searching for their planes prior to a launch, they have frequently noticed one of our more active troubleshooters, with his receding hairline, tattered grey flotation jacket and "GRIT" stenciled on his flight deck helmet, feverishly changing tires or helping push the air cart around the flight deck (the one with the clever square-wheel design). This would be none other than Paul Eddie Samanie, our head troubleshooter and walking chamber of commerce for the sportsman's Paradise of Louisiana. Grit hails from the city of Houma, Louisiana, about 50 miles west of New Orleans, where he graduated from Terrebone High School in 1967. Among the more pleasant memories he holds of home are Bass Fishing, Rabbit and Duck Hunting, and of course Mardi Gras week in Nearby New Orleans.

While in High School Paul worked as an apprentice butcher, but was unable to pursue this specialty when he joined the Navy in September '67 because the only ratings open were in aviation. After completing his boot camp at NTC San Diego, Samanie went to AMS 'A' school in Memphis where he learned the finer points of metalsmithing. This was followed by the usual 8 weeks of F-8 training in VF-124, after which he joined the Red Lightnings aboard the Ticonderoga in June of '68. He worked in the airframes shop for about a year and a half, and was then rewarded with the prestige appointment to troubleshooter.

Grit now resides with his wife Gale and daughter Tyra in San Diego. He plans to leave the Navy in September of '71 and use his VA benefits to obtain a commercial pilots license. With this in hand he plans to work for the J. Ray McDermote Const. Co. making "COD" runs to the oil rigs off the Louisiana Coast.

Since coming to the line Grit has been an outstanding troubleshooter, a leader, and a fine example to his contemporaries. It's a pleasure to recognise him as the RLI's troubleshooter in the spotlight for this issue.

Stepping foward on the hangar deck to recieve his plaque and congratulations from the skipper during our transit between Hong Kong and Cubi Pt. was July's Plane Captain of the month, David Eugene Lantz. Lantz, a 19-year old ASE AN from Sayre, Pennsylvania, has been a standout as plane captain and assistant yellow-gear supervisor since joining the Red Flashes last March. His conscientious application and hard work contributed significantly to availability and reliability of our ground support equipment before we deployed, and since becoming a qualified plane captain back at Miramar his aircraft, 205, has stood out as one of the cleanest and best cared for in the squadron.

-12-

173

Dave's Navy career is a bit different from most in that he never went
to 'A' school. After graduating from Sayre Area High School in 1968 he
went to boot camp at the Great Lakes then went to VF-124 via a two month
stint at NAS Whidbey Island, which was apparently the result of a Navy
SNAFU. During his first nine months with the Gunfighters he was TAD as
a barracks cleaner or mess cook, which together with his time in the
first lieutenants division at Whidbey gave him an unheard of 11 months
in 1st Lt. type jobs. After finally breaking out of this onerous specialty he got into ground support equipment, which was what he really liked.
He had gained wide practical automotive experince while working in
various gas stations in high school.

"Lancer's" wife's name is Cathy; they will have been married a year in
October. After he returns to civilian life in November, '72 he plans
to go right back into public service as a state trooper in either California or New York. To help prepare for this, Dave plans to attend night school in criminoloty during the up coming turnaround (if he can stay off night
check, that is).

As favorite pastimes Dave lists horseback riding, camping, and almost
any kind of sports. He was a varsity letterman in high school in football (offensive halfback) and track (100 yard dash, 220).

Plane Captain of the Month is certainly no mean accomplishment in an
outfit as competitive as the Red Flash line, but Lantz is certainly a deserving recipient of the honor. Keep up the good work.

-13-

R.L.I. STAFF

The Advisor

The Editor

Assistant Editor

The Staff Artist

The RED LIGHTNING ILLUSTRATED is published periodically by the Legendary Red Lightning of Fighter Squadron ONE HUNDRED NINETY FOUR and is a product of the Public Affairs Office in conjunction with the Admin Office.

STAFF		CONTRIBUTORS
ADVISOR:	LTJG J.C. JOHNSON	LT Rocky ROCKWELL
EDITOR:	YN2 David K. BOWMAN	AMS2 Sandy SANDERS
ASS'T		AMH3 Bill RICKWALD
EDITOR:	AO2 T.L. HAND	AO3 Larry WAUTLET
ARTIST:	ATN3 Gary L. MCKISSICK	AE3 Jeff MAGNER
TYPIST:	SA Rade HALL	

Volume II Number 3 SEP-OCT 1970   A RED LIGHTNING PUBLICATION

-14-

175

David K. Bowman

Picture Credits

USS ORISKANY in Alameda: courtesy of www.Glewis.US.

U.S. Naval Activity DaNang, courtesy www.flickr.com.

China Fleet Club, courtesy www.flickr.com

USS ORISKANY sinking, courtesy of:
http://www.lesoleildelafloride.com/Vol27/314-2/Actualites/actualite_USS_OriskanyS

USS ORISKANY underwater: source unknown.

All other photos were taken by the author.

Other Books by
David K. Bowman

LEGERDEMAIN is available through most book sites on the web and order through any book store. Also visit the following sites for more information:
www.sagabooks.net
www.davidkbowman.com
Price: $18.95
Published by Saga Books
474 pages

This award-winning book placed as a Finalist in the 2008 National Best Books competition and is the first book to bring together all the significant facts regarding the disappearance of Amelia Earhart in one volume. Earlier books have concentrated on a particular theory and have only presented a partial picture of the mystery.

Covered in LEGERDEMAIN are:

- The psychic abilities of Amelia Earhart
- The secret cruise of the Nourmahal
- Connection with the disappearance of the Hawaii Clipper
- The truth behind Paul Mantz' Electra
- The Putnam papers
- The bizarre mystery of Wilbur Rothar
- The cryptic telegram from George Huxford
- The startling account of Robert Myers
- The messages in a bottle found in Soulac-sur-Mer, France in 1938

LEGERDEMAIN also contains an exclusive new disclosure.

In addition, LEGERDEMAIN is profusely illustrated with footnotes, bibliography and numerous fact-filled appendices, making it a reference volume to be returned to for years.

Get your copy today!

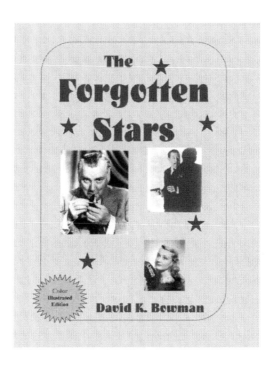

A showcase of Dave's lifelong love of film, this book is the product of five years of research. Many of the biographical articles on old-time actors were published in magazines such as FILMFAX, CULT MOVIES, and SCARLET STREET. Some have never been published, although all of them are in their original versions. Available through Amazon Create Space in an economical printed version with black & white illustrations or a more expensive version with color illustrations. Also available through Amazon Kindle in a color illustrated eBook version.

David K. Bowman

David K. Bowman